JOHN PAUL II

IOHANNES PAULUS

JAN PAWEL

JOHANNES PAUL

JUAN PABLO

JOHN

JEAN PAUL

GIOVANNI PAOLO

JANEZ PAVEL

JÁNOS PÁL

JOÃO PAULO

GJONI-PÁL

JONAS PAULIUS

PAUL II

A PICTORIAL BIOGRAPHY

BY

PETER HEBBLETHWAITE

AND

LUDWIG KAUFMANN

WITH THE COLLABORATION OF:

DR. ALOIS ANKLIN AND DR. REINHOLD LEHMANN

McGRAW-HILL BOOK COMPANY

NEW YORK   SAN FRANCISCO   ST. LOUIS

CONTENTS

A McGraw-Hill Co-Publication

Library of Congress Cataloging in Publication Data. Main entry under title:
John Paul II: a pictorial biography.
Includes index.
1. John Paul II, Pope, 1920–
2. Popes—Biography.
I. Hebblethwaite, Peter.
II. Kaufmann, Ludwig.
BX1378.5.J63   262'.13'0924 [B]
79-9169

ISBN 0-07-033327-0
ISBN 0-07-033328-9 pbk.

Original Concept and Design by:
EMIL M. BUEHRER

Editor:
DAVID BAKER

Managing Editor:
FRANCINE PEETERS

Picture Procuration:
ROSARIA PASQUARIELLO

Production Manager:
FRANZ GISLER

Printed and bound by:
MILANOSTAMPA, FARIGLIANO, ITALY

Composition by:
EDV + FILMSATZ AG,
THUN, SWITZERLAND

Photolithography by:
HEGO AG, LITTAU, SWITZERLAND

Printed in Italy

FOREWORD

The election and investiture of a new pope are "media events" today, broadcast to millions worldwide. In a secularized age such as ours, this public interest in a Church event is surprising, especially when we consider that the pope speaks only for Roman Catholics, who represent one church among many others. Yet the world contains no comparable institution, so universal in extent, with such a long, uninterrupted history. Among the nearly three thousand Catholic bishops in the world today, as well as among the heads of all the other Christian churches, the Bishop of Rome holds a unique office. His powers derive from Christ's direct commands to the Apostle Peter.

How is this office to be executed today, and in the future? "We have to shake off the dust that, since the time of Constantine, has been accumulating on St. Peter's throne." Ever since John XXIII spoke these liberating words during the Vatican Council, the Petrine Ministry has been the object of many theological studies and ecumenical talks—not least within the Anglican community. But when a pope dies, and this came to pass twice in the autumn of 1978, then the cardinals are designated in the name of the Diocese of Rome and the world Church to choose a successor: Whom should they elect, and whom must they not elect? But once the new pope is chosen, all theoretical questions are pushed aside; interest seems to focus, at this point, on the man's nature and origins, his first steps and projects. And the more unknown he was before, the more remote his birthplace, the more modest his family circumstances, and the like, then all the more will people be fascinated by the path that led him to the highest office.

In the case of the present pope, this path coincides with the history of his people for the last sixty years, while his struggles and hardships are bound up with a national history which, though pursued on the margin of the "western world," concerns all of us in both East and West. Unlike his Italian predecessors in this office, he did not spend his youth in the sheltered religious sphere: he was much more involved in what his people were going through—as student, as worker, as actor. . . .

This early history is the subject treated in both word and picture in the first half of the present book. Though there is certainly no lack of pictures of this pope, and much has already been reported concerning his antecedents, still the composite picture-biography formula offers many correlations that allow us better to understand the pope's personality.

The second half of the book presents the beginning of his pontificate, as well as the two important journeys, to Mexico and to Poland. The first of these travels led the pope into a world wholly new to him, where he had to express himself in a language that he had just learned for the occasion, and where he was dependent on the information and evaluations that came to him through the Vatican's diplomatic and bureaucratic channels and perhaps from his contacts with individual bishops and cardinals. In Poland all this was changed, in fact reversed. Here the pope was coming home. Here all the Roman advisers had to take a back seat. For here he knew whom he was addressing, whom he was challenging, and whom he was treating with respect. Here spontaneity and improvisation came into play. The pope on his own: only *here* could one know him as he really is.

To report on the pope's Poland trip, Peter Hebblethwaite flew to Warsaw. The diverse contacts he has maintained through the years in Poland were also helpful to him in the writing of the chapters on Wojtyła's childhood and youth. And thus this colleague in the field of religious journalism, whom I have known since the Vatican Council, joined me as co-author of this work.

Where Latin America is concerned, I myself was present to cover the trip to Mexico and its relationship with the Bishops' Conference at Puebla in January 1979.

Any Catholic who has reached a certain ripeness of age can recall the times, particularly where the papacy was concerned, when the *office* was said to be all that mattered, whereas the individual person, indeed all "human" elements, were secondary. Such a witness of earlier times is surely astounded today to see how this new pope throws his personal style into the balance. And the nonchalance with which John Paul II has *personalized* the papacy—above all in the case of his Poland trip—has provoked diverse reactions. Some persons are relieved that the man no longer hides behind a stiff façade, that he allows human contact to disrupt ritual, that he approaches people fearlessly and will give credit for openness to those who are strict ideological adherents of the East Bloc. Other persons voice concern that all this showmanship might wear the man out, and that the nonstop "happenings" and appearances may reduce the pope to a dimestore commodity in the media consumer market. Everyone knows how short-lived is the "hero" whose virility, charm, or seductiveness fascinates the masses, and how quickly this enthusiasm can turn sour. Even the history of the papacy offers some object-lessons in this regard. One has only to think back a hundred years to Pio Nono, Pius IX!

What prompts me, in the midst of the universal enthusiasm, to register such concern and such surprise, is simply the sympathy aroused by my first meeting with the then Cardinal Wojtyła. I met him, all alone, in the middle of a square in the Vatican. It was in the autumn of 1974, immediately after the conclusion of a Bishops' Synod. For Cardinal Wojtyła the Synod had not turned out as he had wanted. In the fulfillment of a papal assignment, he had exerted himself literally day and night, along with some others, in the drafting of a "Concluding Statement." Having wasted his words, he now stood there cheerful nevertheless, his arms crossed, pleased with the sunshine, giving brief, direct answers to my questions. I had the impression: here is a man at peace with himself. The same spontaneous feeling was prompted on the occasion of his first appearance as newly elected pope on the balcony of St. Peter's. Facing the applauding crowd, he supported himself with his arms against the balustrade and simply waited, avoiding any other gesture, until the noise had subsided below.

It irritates me now to see this man—who had so impressed me with his independence and his restraint—suddenly plastered all over billboards and Church magazine covers like some TV personality.

It is not possible for me here to explore the questions touching upon the ecumenical accommodation that might be made possible by such a personalization. In ecumenical circles, no less than in other spheres, one can only rejoice over such a pronounced "charisma" and specifically over the courage in the defense of human rights and human dignity in the face of totalitarian regimes. And it can surely do no harm within the Catholic Church if her bureaucratic apparatus (swollen more than ever in the last years) is shoved to the background, and its officials on all levels are brought face to face with a living example of how one can seek contact with people, without fear, and thus give the Church a "human face."

But it would be something else again if, as some fear, this personalization were to become a "Polanization." This pope gives us the long overdue chance to revise the frozen western conception of "Europe," in order to embrace the membership of the "East," which is a fact of some thousand years' standing. But to expect the salvation of the whole Church according to a Polish "model" would be to overlook just how unique a case the pope's country is in history and in the present. The fact that we admire the Polish Church and that we pay her her due recognition does not necessarily mean that we ought to cite her as a certain conception of "discipline" and "decisiveness" or as the epitome of a moral rigor (which is also unjustified by the facts).

The Catholic Church is of course *in* the world and has to serve the cause of peace; it must, in all earnestness—as the new Vatican secretary of state Cardinal Casaroli has said—contribute to the easing of tensions between East and West in the person of its new pope, though he has rarely so far been an element in this thawing. But the Church also faces the problems of her own "unity in diversity." No euphoria, no spectacular journeys, can erase these problems, as in fact the papal official newspaper so conspicuously remarked on the pope's return from Poland.

The newspaper cited as an example the "acculturation" of Christianity, meaning a process of naturalization in the various cultures, in each new generation, and so on. It is in this long view that a solution to such problems must be sought: there are moments for adjustment, for the setting of new sights, when a new mentality has a chance to break through (or conversely is denied its chance), and it is quite possible that this is true most of all in the dynamic of a new pontificate. And so it seems to me that a sense of critical alertness is called for. The pope who calls again and again for "collegiality," and thus for shared responsibility, is surely the last person who wants to become the opiate and the alibi for closing our eyes to the autonomous possibilities of the communities "whose time has come." In this sense one might prefer in certain media to have "less pope" and more *eglesia de base*—more "grassroots Christianity."

On the cover of this book the pope is seen holding up a small Latin American Indian boy. To me this lad symbolizes the dominant generation which, by the time the third millennium begins, must be capable of assuming responsibility. This perspective, offered occasionally in this book, may serve as our hope for the future.

Ludwig Kaufmann

THE SECRET CONCLAVE

What went on, from 14 to 16 October 1978, behind the walls and locked doors that isolated the College of Cardinals from the world outside? There are no published minutes on the meeting, and indeed the cardinals were obliged to burn their personal notes on the deliberations, together with their actual ballots, in the "stove" of the Sistine Chapel. Such was the strict regulation on papal conclaves, as handed down since the Middle Ages and tightened still further by Pope Paul VI himself. What little we know about the motives and intentions of the cardinals—and it is little indeed—is based on sporadic comments uttered before the conclave began. "It is absolutely sure," we were told, that the cardinals would elect "another pastor of souls" who could establish contact with people. The word "another" here is a reference to the man they had elected at the end of the preceding August: "the smiling Pope Luciani—John Paul I." The happy man from the Veneto was crushed to death by the flood of tasks and the burden of responsibility in the short thirty-three days of his office. More than a few persons, moreover, found it painful to have the whole ritual of a papal election played out yet again, for the second time in two months (Paul VI had died on 6 August, John Paul I on 28 September). Everything had the appearance of a carbon copy. Was there any way the new pope could avoid being just a papier-mâché "second Luciani" and/or a second-choice candidate?

On Sunday evening (15 October) more than 100,000 eager witnesses gathered in St. Peter's Square received the disappointing signal—black smoke from the Sistine Chapel—indicating that no candidate had as yet gained the necessary votes (two-thirds of the cardinals plus one). But twenty-four hours later the task was complete. White smoke, this time, brought joy and relief to the faithful in the great square, and to those all over the world, who had prayed for a favorable election. They were convinced that the man chosen by the cardinals was the man God wanted. But who was he?

In the solemn tradition of the conclave, one hundred eleven cardinals came together in October 1978—for the second time in two months—to elect a pope in the Sistine Chapel.

A POPE FOR THE YEAR 2000?

Pericle Felici, Cardinal Deacon of the Roman Church, hesitated when, from the high balcony of St. Peter's, he was about to announce the name of the new pope to the hundred thousand people standing in the huge square below. Not that he was to utter it for the first time, but until then everyone had pronounced the name his own way, perhaps with the stress on the first syllable. This time it had to sound authentic. And so the Roman paused in the sonorous flow of the Latin announcement formula ("Annuntio vobis...Habemus Papam...Carolum...cardinalem...") and, shifting the stress to the *Y* and pursing his lips, tried to produce the Slavic sound *ł* (similar to our *W*) Below, in the square, people cast about at the exotic (Asiatic? African?) sounds: *Voi-Tüwa*. Who was that? It took some seconds until, from the transistor-recorded comments of Radio Vatican, the announcement became clear to all. Now it dawned: the new pope was a Pole. The surprise on that Monday evening was threefold. First, a non-Italian. Since 1522 the cardinals had never resorted to such an alternative. But this time, on the evening of the first day of their conclave—after four ballots—it became clear that they had not been able to settle on an Italian candidate with the necessary two-thirds majority (exactly: two-thirds plus one). It is a fair guess that the Italians could not agree among themselves. However, no reliable information is available on the actual proceedings. All participants are under a strict pledge of secrecy, and so the proceedings within the conclave remain sealed. Yet during the days before, several cardinals had been relatively communicative; indeed, there had even been a press campaign, in favor of an Italian candidate and against another—an event without precedent in recent papal election history. It was the Archbishop of Genoa, Cardinal Siri, who, in a press interview, brought the dispute to a head. After its (premature) publication on the morning when the conclave was to begin, it was a foregone conclusion that at any rate that Italian candidate, who would have turned the wheel of history back beyond the Council to Pius XII, his one-time sponsor, had lost out. What was less certain was whether his counterpart, Cardinal Benelli, who had been closely associated with the post-Conciliar reign of Paul VI and his curial administration, would fail at a stub-

born blockade group. What was not foreseeable at all was that disagreement would deprive all the other candidates of the Italian peninsula of any chance, and that the man would have to be sought elsewhere.

But that the choice should finally fall on a Pole—that was the second and by far greater sensation. Never in the long record of papal history had this happened, and hardly anyone would have believed that the senate of the Roman Church would undertake the "geopolitical" risk of fetching the new pope from a Communist state.

The third surprise was Wojtyła's comparatively low age of fifty-eight. Only two months before, after the passing of Paul VI (1963–1978), sixty-five had seemed the minimum age for one eligible to the papal throne. There had been misgivings at the prospect of a long pontificate. Now, under the shock of the early death of John Paul I—who, at sixty-six, died after only thirty-three days in office—the cardinals seem to have inclined toward a personality of comparatively youthful vigor and robust nature.

So it might not be so farfetched to predict a reign for the new pope extending to the dawn of the third millennium. Born in May 1920, he may, even if he resigns at eighty (the new age limit to eligibility of the cardinals), still be in office in the year 2000.

However, the real issue is not one of the calendar or of *chronos,* but rather one of *kairos:* What kind of future lies ahead for mankind, and what are the signs of this future? What chances exist for the Gospel, and "what plans does the Lord have for His Church?"

Pope Wojtyła himself, when taking office, posed the question; but he did not claim to have an answer, not for the "next years" even. "God knows," he said, meaning that he would be guided neither by apocalyptic visions of the future nor by set formulas. The question as to God's intentions, whether it may be granted us to divine them, is only a hope expressed in humility.

Still, at the risk of being immodest, we might ask what outlines emerge for Church and Christendom for the year 2000. Certain *geopolitical* trends may be inferred from demographic statistics and their application to the population of the faithful. By the end of this century, the numbers will no longer be with Europe. For the Catholics, at least, *Latin America* will rank first, followed by *Africa*. It could have been reasonable to expect the first non-Italian pope to come from either of those continents, in view of the future trends and the shifting emphasis. And after the preceding Bishops' Synods there had been no lack of "eligibles" from the Third World being discussed prior to the conclave. And as none of them was elected pope, it might be fair to ask: Did the majority of the cardinals fail to look into the future? Did they not see the "Third Church at the Gates," as a striking book title, recalling Hannibal's threat to Rome, had proclaimed in Rome's shop windows back in 1974? Did they close their eyes to the pressing new challenges and inspiring impulses emanating from the Third World? From Africa comes the theme of acculturation (or the naturalization of the Gospel in different cultures);; from Asia, the issue of the non-Christian religions, their role in God's intentions, and their relation to the religious history of the Jewish-Christian Bible; from Latin America, the call for "integral liberation," meaning evangelization acting as a catalyst in the liberation process of oppressed people and at the same time giving that process meaning and inspiration.

In 1974, at the Bishops' World Synod in Rome, those topics were voiced, resulting in a survey of the various continents such as had never before been undertaken by an official body of the Church. And the permanent council of the Bishops' Synod was more or less elected according to continents or cultural areas. Immediately thereafter, all Roman newsstands displayed a large placard, with luminous yellow lettering on a black ground: "Hanno eletto il prossimo papa"—"At the Bishops' Synod they elected the next pope." For the moment it was a mere gag, but today we might see it as intuition. Among those elected there, the fourth name (after Lorscheider for Latin America, Etchegaray for Europe, and Zoa for Africa) was Karol Wojtyła, Number 2 for Europe. At the Synod, he had held an official function as pope-appointed reporter on the theological aspects of the topic "evangelization"—a function which, in the complicated and rather inefficient working procedure of that event, was not exactly a rewarding task, especially as he had to share it with a consul-

tant, the Roman professor D. Grasso. Some quarters even spoke of a failure, with the criticism that Wojtyła's theology floated above the clouds and relied on abstract principles instead of on the hard facts of history. If he nevertheless gained a seat—outscoring, for instance, the fiery Asian Cordeiro (Pakistan) by 36 votes (at the 1971 Synod, Cordeiro had had a lead of some 20 votes on Wojtyła in both elections)—the reason may be that he had collaborated on the continental survey of the Third World mentioned above.

Even ten years before, as a young bishop at the Council, Wojtyła had made some remarkable and still topical addresses on religious freedom and on the dialogue with atheism, and then, referring to the proposal n the Church in the "world of today," appropriately pointed out that the Church was in fact dealing with "several worlds." On that occasion also, he spoke out against representing the Church solely as an instructress, as if the world were humbly at her feet; the real issue, he said, was "*jointly* to *search* for a true and just solution to the difficult problems of man's life."

If this is still the conviction of the pope today and if the insights gained at the Bishops' Synod still influence his thought, we may hope, in the light of his own words, that he will accept variety and pluralism within the Church also and will give greater effect to the principle of good fellowship by reducing bureaucratic centralism. And if Europe today is now merely the "baroque balcony" of the world's edifice, as someone has said, it is clear that Rome can no longer claim to be the center of the world.

The new pope, appearing on the balcony of St. Peter's half an hour after the solemn announcement, told the Romans that he had "come from far off," but had always been near to them in the faith. Would it not be appropriate for every Catholic in Europe to reconsider what is near and far, and seek to overcome the familiar notion of concentric circles wheeling round one center? For, to see Church and pope in such comfortable terms is an anachronism for a Christian in the larger world of today, and would be even more so in the year 2000.

JOHN PAUL THE SECOND

*The investiture, in St. Peter's Square: the transformation of Polish cardinal Karol Wojtyła into the Bishop of Rome and pope of the worldwide Catholic Church. The process, begun with the selection of his new name, was completed by the donning of papal vestments and the white cap (*pileolum*). Finally, the so-called pallium or stole was placed around his shoulders—symbolizing the rank and duties of the "Metropolitan," as bishops of major cities in East and West have been called since the early Middle Ages.*

The new pope's rather formal and ponderous double name, which he took over from his predecessor, seems less and less appropriate to his personal, combative style as the months go by. The gesture of choosing this name was of course understandable, at a time when everyone was still stunned by the sudden disappearance of the smiling Pope Luciani. But since then it has become increasingly clear just how different the two men are in temperament and character.

In any case the new pope is not afraid to be himself and to remain himself. Perhaps the best way to represent his real nature is to stick to his old civilian name and refer to him simply as Pope Wojtyła.

It has been an unbroken tradition, for the last thousand years or so, for a pope to choose a new name when he is elected. There were several reasons for this custom. In some cases the old name sounded too pagan or "barbarian," in other cases it was perhaps too "holy." Twice in the tenth century, men were elected pope who had the given name Peter. Both of them considered it unseemly to use this name as pope. In fact, neither before then nor since, has there ever been a Pope Peter—for the Roman Catholic Church considers Peter the Apostle to be Number 1 in the long list of her 266 popes. Every pope is essentially a successor.

But in the choice of his papal name, each man can still indicate his desire to adopt a specific model, to continue a particular tradition, or at least to bend a tradition in a new direction. Thus the year 1958 marked the end of the "Pius" era, and the new pope's choice of the name John XXIII made it clear that he was reverting back to early history, beyond the papacy of the whole modern era. Paul VI was guided in his selection of a name by his partiality for the Apostle Paul. Like St. Peter, Paul preached in Rome and was martyred in this city, but in his missionary travels he represents a contrast to the "sedentary" Peter; and Paul VI apparently would have liked to incorporate both these vocations in himself—both the conquest of the faith and its preservation. On assuming the pontificate, however, he spoke first of all about his three immediate predecessors, Pius XI, Pius XII, and John XXIII, whom he hoped to emulate.

John Paul II, unlike his immediate predecessor, made no specific allusion to his chosen name during his inaugural homily. But factually, far more than formally, John Paul "the Second" emphasized the theme expressed by "the First" when choosing his double name—he stressed, above all, *continuity* with the two popes of the second Vatican Council (1962–1965). Indeed, among his major concerns Pope Wojtyła cited the desire to translate the Council and its implications into specific acts and thereby to be in tune with life, with history. In this connection he had particular praise for the Catholic bishops' concrete realization of collegial shared responsibility, in the form of the periodic Bishops Synods in recent years.

His emphasis of this theme was especially significant because the conclave had been marked by a challenge, and in fact a threat, to the Council in general and to collegiality in particular. If part of this collegial outlook means that the cultural diversity of the so-called local and regional churches should be given greater play, it would certainly have done no harm to enrich the list of papal names with a completely new one indicating the pope's own origins. Some people wondered why Wojtyła, the former archbishop of Kraków, did not name himself after his famous predecessor in that post, St. Stanislas. It is even said that he at first flirted with this idea and then—perhaps out of respect for the Italians, perhaps on Cardinal Wyszyński's advice—gave it up.

Be that as it may, there were good reasons for rejecting this name—including historical reasons: there is some question now whether Poland's patron saint was really condemned to death. But there is no question that Bishop Stanislas came into conflict with the secular government of his day. So the name Pope Stanislas I could have been taken as a challenge to the Polish government.

THE YEAR 1920

In 1920, year of the pope's birth, the Polish Republic was only two years old and Warsaw, its capital (right), was besieged by the Red Army from across the Vistula River. The Soviets were defeated in the "miracle of the Vistula," 15 August 1920, and driven off of Polish soil.

But the young state's troubles did not all come from outside. Internal disharmony, party strife, and economic difficulties in the early 1920s led to a crisis. Power was seized in 1926 by the war hero Marshal Jozef Piłsudski (left), who ruled until his death in 1935.

Karol Wojtyła was born on 18 May 1920 at Wadowice in Galicia, the southern province of Poland. The independence of Poland had been proclaimed only a year and a half before, on 11 November 1918. For over a century the country had been carved up between its more powerful neighbors, Russia, Prussia, and Austria. Now at last they were free to start rebuilding their war-ravaged country. Thanks to the language, the culture, and the Church, the sense of "nationhood" had been preserved throughout the long period of partition; now the nation could become a "state" once more.

Independence, however, brought many problems. The infant state was already at war with the Soviet Union, and only three months after Wojtyła was born, the Red Army stood at the gates of Warsaw. It was flung back at the last moment in a historic battle known as "the miracle of the Vistula." The battle was finally won on the feast of the Assumption of Our Lady. Patriotic enthusiasm knew no bounds.

But patriotism was no substitute for a policy. It proved less easy to reintegrate Poles into one nation than the romantic dreams had suggested. Political divisions were inherited from the period of partition. There were the middle-class National Democrats, intensely nationalistic and socially conservative, whose main strength lay in the former Prussian regions of the West. The Piast wing of the Polish Peasant movement was particularly strong in Galicia, where Wojtyła was born. Socialism had flourished in the former Russian territories. Marshal Józef Piłsudski began as a Socialist, but then abandoned Socialism and carried many of his followers with him. After the war with Russia the Communist party was banned and remained illegal throughout the lifetime of the republic. Grave economic difficulties did not help a country that was still predominantly agricultural. In 1925 Germany denounced her trade treaty with Poland, causing a serious crisis in the Polish coal industry, on which the country depended. In the confusion, Piłsudski decided to act, marched on Warsaw in May 1926, replaced the president by his own nominee, and proceeded to rule until his death in May 1935. He was officially mourned by the whole nation as her greatest modern statesman, though there were also some dissident voices. Thereafter the country was ruled by the "government of colonels" who had to face a new and increasingly menacing version of the old Polish dilemma: wedged between two powerful neighbors, Germany and Soviet Russia, in which direction should they turn? And could they, in the event of trouble, expect help from the West?

Below: *Following the defeat of the Soviets and their retreat from the Vistula, the two countries met in 1921 at Riga, on the Baltic Sea, for a peace conference in which the Soviet Union was obliged to yield considerable territory. Thus were established the borders that would remain in effect until World War II. Already in 1922 a German general was promising Poland's eventual destruction "by her own internal weaknesses, and by Russia—with German help."*

Another factor complicated the situation still further. Though Catholicism had shaped the nation, it did not have a monopoly in post-1920 Poland. To the east there were many Orthodox Christians, Lutheran communities existed in the west, and ten percent of the population was Jewish.

In these circumstances of fragility and division, it was natural that many Poles should turn to the past to compensate for the distressing present. They could remember the conversion to Christianity of Mieszko I, prince of the Piast dynasty, in 996. They could recall the glories of the cathedral at Gniezno where the first Polish kings had been crowned: to this day, the Polish primate still has the title of Archbishop of Gniezno. There were different memories in Kraków. In the sixteenth century it had been the capital of Poland, economic life expanded, and the country was militarily strong (Polish armies even occupied Moscow from 1610 to 1612). Artists and scholars flocked to Kraków. Though the Counter-Reformation triumphed in Poland, the country was at this time more tolerant than most countries of Western Europe. After notable victories over a new invader—Sweden—in the seventeenth century, Poland went into decline and was ripe for plucking by the time of the first partition of 1772. There was a brief flurry of hope with the Constitution of 1791, but it was quickly extinguished, and the second partition of 1793 led to a

whole century of bloody revolts and bitter disappointments. In 1920 in Warsaw the heavy guns of the Citadel which had housed the Russian garrison still pointed not outward but inward toward the heart of the city. And there was also the Brama Straceń, the execution gate where condemned Poles were left to hang struggling on the end of a rope, till they died.

It has never been easy to be Polish. A combination of bad luck, economic backwardness, geo-politics, and internal dissensions meant that tragedy has never been far away. This was true in the year 1920 when Wojtyła was born and when the country embarked on its twentieth-century experiment in independence.

THE WOJTYŁA FAMILY

On 10 February 1906, Karol Wojtyła, a noncommissioned administrative officer in the Austro-Hungarian army, married Emilia Kaczorowska, a young Silesian of Lithuanian origin. For their second son, Karol junior, the family history was a symbolic reminder of the period of Polish-Lithuanian unity in rebellion against Russia in the nineteenth century. As pope, Wojtyła addressed a particularly warm greeting to the Lithuanians.

Karol Wojtyła's paternal grandfather, Maciej, was a tailor in the village of Czaniec, near Andrychów, south of Kraków. Other ancestors are buried in the churchyard of Czaniec. Many years later Cardinal Wojtyła preached a sermon in a nearby church and spoke with pride of his forefathers who had led pilgrimages to Calvary, one of the most famous shrines of Poland.

His father, also called Karol, had served in the Austro-Hungarian Imperial army, and by the time of his birth was an administrative officer in the Polish army. His mother, Emilia (née Kaczorowska), was a schoolteacher whose parents came from Silesia. The couple already had one child, Edmund, who was fifteen in 1920. They had settled in Wadowice after their marriage.

Wadowice was, and remains, a small town where everyone knew everyone else. The tragedies which struck the Wojtyła family are still recalled there. It knew hardship, for Karol senior had retired from the army on a small pension. When Karol junior was nearly nine, his mother died at the age of forty-five, giving birth to a still-born girl. Karol (he was always known as "Lolek") was not altogether deprived of feminine company by this loss—he became very attached to his godmother, who still lives in Kraków; but it is not fanciful to trace his devotion to Our Lady from this early experience. In his letter to priests dated Palm Sunday 1979, he wrote: "I desire that all of you priests should find in Mary the Mother of the priesthood which we have received from Christ." He added that this was based on his own experience.

Three years after the death of Emilia, Edmund, who had qualified as a doctor and was working in a hospital at Bielsko, caught scarlet fever from one of his patients and died. Lolek was now alone with his father. Karol senior was a military man through and through and a strict disciplinarian. Every day had its program: Mass, school, an hour's free time, then homework. But he was also warm-hearted and well-read. He pinned all his hopes on Lolek, his only surviving child. They had a good relationship. Wojtyła's vocation—which no one thought about at the time—does not conform to the classic pattern of a pious mother balanced by an absent or dissolute father.

Karol had gone to the Boys' High School (*gimnasjum*) in 1931. He remained intensely loyal to the friends he made there. Until 1978 he used to invite his twenty-two surviving classmates to a reunion in the Archbishop's Palace in Kraków. One of them was a young Jew called Kluger. He and his family had one of the first private audiences after Wojtyła became pope.

One of his teachers, Fr. Zacher, recalls Karol the schoolboy: "I was sent to teach religion at the High School in Wadowice in December 1932. I remember one of my first classes....There was a boy with a sad, intelligent face, and afterwards I asked the others who he was. 'It's Lolek Wojtyła,' they said, and explained that he was sad because his only brother had just died." Fr. Zacher went on to teach Wojtyła for the next six years. He says bluntly: "He was the nearest to a genius that I ever taught." The young Wojtyła was particularly good at languages, ancient and modern. He was less good at physics and chemistry. He reveled in philosophy in his later years.

However, none of the witnesses suggest that Lolek was wholly immersed in his books or that he was a prig. He loved sport, proved a tough and relentless goalkeeper, and loved to swim in the flood waters of the River Skawa. But most of all he loved skiing, which took him to the not too distant mountains—Wadowice itself is merely in the foothills. But the mountains with their terrible beauty, their physical challenge, and their sturdily independent people, helped to shape his outlook. A doctor who knew him well says: "He comes from the foothills, not from the mountains; but he *belongs* with the mountain people. He loves their songs and poetry: he shares their simplicity, their sense of humor, their independence, their love of freedom. The mountain people have never been serfs, so they symbolize the equality that exists between man and man; they have always been in love with freedom."

The pope's father, like his grandfather, had set out to be a tailor. But in the fall of 1900 he was drafted into the Austro-Hungarian army, assigned to an infantry regiment stationed in Wadowice, and soon promoted. The group picture above shows him (center) in a card game with fellow noncommissioned officers. He was considered serious-minded and mature, with a strong sense of duty.

Promoted as a noncommissioned officer in accounting, he spent the beginning of World War I in the administrative offices where he proved his worth. He won the iron service medal with crown and in 1915 was promoted to the officer corps. The new Polish republic, after the war, made him a lieutenant (picture at left).

Right: Portrait of young Mrs. Wojtyła from the period before Karol's birth.

Overleaf (pp. 20–21): The parents are shown with young Karol, around 1922–1923. Their third child, a girl, was still-born, and the mother died giving birth to her, at forty-five years of age.

WADOWICE:
BIRTHPLACE OF THE FUTURE POPE

On the second floor of this house, at number 7 Church Street, Karol grew up. He was born on another street, but his parents moved here soon thereafter. Like most houses in Wadowice, this modest building is only adorned with the papal colors in honor of John Paul II. The diocese of Kraków would like to purchase the building and make it a museum, but the owner is absent: he lives in Israel.

The market town of Wadowice, 30 kilometers (20 miles) from Kraków, grew to a population of 10,000 during the eighteen years that Karol Wojtyła lived there. Its market featured local agricultural produce, especially wheat, potatoes, and beets. Wadowice was also a garrison town, and Wojtyła senior made his mark in its military administration. The town's most impressive building by far is the classical Baroque parish church with its onion-dome. In this church Karol was baptized, received his first communion, and served as an altar boy, and here he celebrated his first mass as a new priest after his return home from his ordination in Kraków. He also came back to visit his hometown as a bishop. This was a particularly festive occasion, in conjunction with the *Millennium Poloniae*—Poland's thousand-year jubilee commemorating the baptism of the first known Polish sovereign, Miesko I, in 966. Wojtyła joined with the whole parish in thanksgiving for the gift of the faith, and in a renewal of their baptismal vows.

Right: *At the news of Wojtyła's election as pope, children gathered at the flower-bedecked baptismal font of the Wadowice parish church. Here Karol was baptized, on 20 May 1920. A commemorative plaque on the wall recalls this date, along with that of the solemn renewal of his baptismal vows on 26 November 1966, in the year of the millennium of Polish Christianity; Wojtyła's elevation to cardinal in June 1967 is also mentioned. But the plaque bears no portrait of the pope; instead it has a relief carving of John the Baptist. The sacrament of baptism establishes the equality of every Christian. During the thousand-year jubilee many members of the Kraków diocese made pilgrimages to their own baptismal churches.*

Opposite: *The proud Baroque façade of the parish church of Wadowice is dedicated to Our Lady. Its tower dominates the city's horizon; it must have had a profound effect on young Karol as he hastened to mass early in the morning.*

THE PERSONALITY

"A great life," said the French poet Alfred de Vigny, "is a dream of youth realized in maturity." Karol Wojtyła's dream took shape slowly, under the pressure of events, both private and public. He was driven by the death of his mother into a closer relationship with his father than most boys experience. After the unexpected death of his brother he became the focus of his father's remaining hopes and ambitions. He was early on drawn to poetry, acting, and the theater as an outlet for his creativity: he would never be a passive spectator of life. His literary interests were nationalistic, which also meant that they were Catholic. Mickiewicz was not the only romantic poet who identified the sufferings of Poland with the passion of Christ. The occupation which began in 1939 made this theme seem more relevant than ever: it offered a possible way of coping with tragedy and also provided a vision of hope for the future.

But though Wojtyła remained interested in literature, it was in philosophy that he came to feel at home. All the psychological features that observers note in him—the strength of conviction, the self-confident optimism, the openness to dialogue, the directness and naturalness in personal relations, his prayerfulness—find their justification in his philosophy. One can either say that his philosophy made him what he was, or that he was drawn to this sort of philosophy because he wanted to become this sort of person. Both statements are true.

He is, for instance, a complete man, an all-rounder. In *The Acting Person* he is greatly concerned to make a complete statement about man, in all his dimensions. He makes room for the body, for the emotional life, for the biological impulses we know so little about, and for the subconscious. He is not afraid of any of these dimensions. There is nothing anxious or neurotic about his personal relationships. He is not reluctant to touch people or to embrace them. He does not regard tears as a form of weakness. His picture of the human person is not of a desiccated, disembodied mind, but of a full-blooded, thinking and feeling, fully alive, complete all-rounder.

It goes without saying that this ideal cannot be attained, either in philosophy or in life, by a single, magical leap. It takes time for virtualities to unfold. For Wojtyła the human being is always *becoming*. It is not ready-made. It builds itself up gradu-ally through its action on the world. Through decisions, choices, commitments. If his philosophy stresses the will, it is not a doctrine of self-mastery for its own sake. For he always sees the will as "a rational appetite" (to use the scholastic term) which means that it is always drawn onward by what is true and good and beautiful. Man's horizon according to Wojtyła is not closed: it opens out continually to the ideals which beckon him on. Hence man's dynamism, to use another of his favorite words.

Moreover, human acts for Wojtyła are never indifferent: either they lead toward the good or they lead away from it. There is no escape from morality. Freedom is the essential condition of a truly human act. It enables a person to become "more himself," to realize his potential, to become ever more lucid, self-possessed, responsible for others, more open to God. This helps to explain why Wojtyła gives the feeling that he is always *wholly himself,* whether he is dealing with a crowd or with individuals. He may have been an actor, but there is nothing feigned or faked about what he says and does. He commits himself, not a part of himself.

We can see here, too, the roots of his strong sense of commitment—whether in marriage or in priestly or religious life. When someone says "I will" consciously, lucidly, and in freedom, they are not merely uttering words that can later be withdrawn: they are staking their lives on the commitment they make. Moreover for Wojtyła these basic commitments or life-choices have an *integrating* role: they gather together all the scattered and disparate actions of a human life and give them meaning and direction. Hence John Paul's constant emphasis on fidelity. He is all of a piece with his philosophy. It is a philosophy directed to action: on himself and on the world. But it also leaves room for passivity, listening, and intuition—in short, for prayer.

Edmund Wojtyła (top) studied medicine. As a young practitioner he became infected with scarlet fever and did not survive. He died in 1932, at age twenty-six.

Above: Young Karol, with close-cropped hair and somewhat protruding ears, on the day of his first communion, dressed in the time-honored festive attire: white suit, white stockings, white shoes. In his right hand he holds the communion candle. On the table beside him stands the first communion remembrance, also in the typical style of Eastern European pious art.

Karol lost his mother before he was nine years old. This picture was taken around that time (1929), shortly before her death. The mother is shown in a fanciful hat, with a handbag. The atmosphere recalls the Austro-Hungarian Empire, even though that state had already ceased to exist. True to his father's example, Karol is wearing the uniform of the Wadowice military school, which his brother Edmund, fourteen years his senior, had also attended. A uniform meant a good deal in the Wojtyła family.

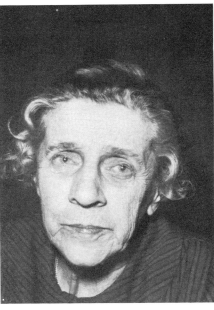

Felicia Wjadrowska (above), daughter of Wojtyła's long since deceased godmother, lived to witness his pontificate.

Left: *As a student, with his godmother Maria Wjadrowska in a Kraków park. Karol had enrolled in the autumn of 1938 in the Jagiellonian University, one of the oldest institutions of higher learning in Europe. He studied Polish language and literature. He had already completed eight years of secondary schooling in the Wadowice* gimnasjum. *The slender little boy from the first communion picture had become by now a tall, broadshouldered man.*

A school excursion to Wieliczka, near Kraków, 26 May 1930. Ten-year-old Karol is in the second row, at far left.

When Cardinal Wojtyła's schoolfriends met for their annual reunion in Kraków, they found him warmhearted and enthusiastic, "just as we always knew him at school." They do not remember that he had ever spoken about becoming a priest at that time. His interests had lain elsewhere, in theater and patriotic literature. His friends remember his performance in a play by Juliusz Słowacki, one of the leading poets of the nineteenth century. Curiously enough, in December 1849, Słowacki had written a poem in which he looked forward to a Slavic pope:

This Pope will not—Italian-like—take fright
At saber thrust
But brave as God himself, stand and give fight—
His world—but dust....
Love he dispenses as great powers today
Distribute arms:
With sacramental power—his sole array—
The World he charms.

Karol (rear, far left) shown with a few of his classmates. In the margin each boy signed his name. Karol was considered an excellent pupil. His grades were "Very Good" in all subjects except history, chemistry, and physics. He had a passion for literature and theater.

KRAKÓW:
AN UNUSUAL CITY

Kraków owes its existence to its position on a bend of the River Vistula and especially to the limestone rock on which stands the Castle of Wawel, residence and burial place of Polish kings until 1609. The cathedral forms part of the complex of buildings that make up the castle. The wrought-iron monogram K beneath a crown commemorates King Kazimierz the Great, the last king of the Piast dynasty in the fourteenth century. Nestling in the shadow of the castle is the city proper, with its Renaissance market place (the Rynek Głowny) and the church of St. Mary in the top right-hand corner. Every hour a trumpeter appears on its tower to mark the time. His trumpet call is always unfinished in memory of a trumpeter long ago who was killed, in full blast, by a Tartar arrow. In 1938 Karol Wojtyła moved to Kraków to begin the study of Polish literature at the Jagiellonian University, which had been founded in 1364 by King Kazimierz and was later supported by Jadwiga, Queen of Poland, who was beatified in the early twentieth century. In its early years, half the university population came from abroad. Its most famous students were the astronomer Nicolas Copernicus, the original of the notorious Dr. Faustus, and from 1912 to 1914 Vladimir Lenin used to come and read in its well-stocked library. The city escaped major destruction in both world wars. It still has something of the atmosphere of the Austro-Hungarian Empire, with its café society and its numerous theaters. It is a relaxed and friendly place, in which the past is not forgotten and in which there is no great sense of urgency or rush. The friars and nuns in their habits move confidently about the narrow Renaissance streets, and one can forget that one is in a Communist country. It is easy to understand why it has been called "the jewel of Poland."

Kraków was Wojtyła's home from 1938, when he first came here to study at the prestigious university, until 1978, when he left his post as cardinal of Kraków to become pope. As a young priest, in 1948, he was assigned to St. Florian's Church in Kraków (right), his second pastoral charge.

Kraków is often called, with good reason, "the jewel of Poland" and her "secret capital." The streets and squares of the old quarter are lined with lovely Renaissance buildings, such as the sixteenth-century Drapers' Guild Hall (above), impressive backdrop to the market square.

Above right: View, through an arch of the Drapers' Hall, of the Church of Our Lady, the largest and probably finest church in Kraków. The Gothic structure was rebuilt around 1400.

Right: Detail from the high-altar sculpture in the Church of Our Lady, which consists of 2,000 painted and gilded wooden figures.

The Wawel castel (left), residence of Poland's kings until 1609, stands alongside the cathedral on a rocky hill in Kraków. During the Nazi occupation this castle was the headquarters of the notorious governor of the Polish territory, General Hans Frank. But in the castle crypt, along with the tombs of Poland's bishops and kings, lay the old poets and minstrels whose songs inspired nationalist resistance.

Religious pageants remain an essential part of the calendar in Communist-governed Poland. Every Good Friday (below left), the monks in a monastery near Kraków reenact, in full costume, the Stations of the Cross.

Below: From the yearly procession to the Christmas crèche in Kraków.

THE YEAR 1939

During the summer of 1939 Wojtyła and his fellow students were in special camps, known as the Academic Legion, where they underwent basic military training. They were home again by mid-August and on 22 August read in their newspapers that Germany and the Soviet Union had concluded a treaty of friendship. That could mean only one thing: Hitler's armies would have a free hand to do what they liked with Poland. The inevitable attack began on 1 September and a new word, *Blitzkrieg,* was used to describe its speed and terror. Cavalry was pitted against tanks, and bombs rained down on the long columns of refugees. By 6 September the German Fourteenth Army had reached Kraków, and two days later the Nazis were in Warsaw. On 17 September the Russians moved in from the East to complete the dismemberment of Poland and to set up yet another partition, bloodier than any that had gone before.

The German authorities in Kraków wasted no time in showing what they intended to do. On 6 November the professors and other teaching staff of the Jagiellonian University were summoned to a meeting ostensibly to discuss its reopening. Only those prudent enough to feign colds or to stay away escaped arrest and despatch to the concentration camp of Sachsenhausen, and though some came back, the majority were never seen again.

Hitler regarded the Poles as a slave race. They had therefore no business to be intellectuals, and the elimination of Polish elites—army officers, professors, educated priests—was a first priority. Hitler's orders to Hans Frank, who was made responsible for the part of Poland which included Kraków, made this perfectly clear: "The Poles are born for low labor.... There can be no question of improvement for them. The standard of living in Poland must be kept low. The priests will preach what we want them to preach. If any priest acts differently, we will make short work of him. The task of priests is to keep the Poles quiet, stupid, and dull-witted."

The travail of Poland had begun. The Nazis were both ruthless and efficient. With insolent irony, Hans Frank installed himself in the Castle of Wawel, and from there directed the work of terror, enslavement, and destruction. Not far away was the concentration camp of Auschwitz, to which Jews were being shunted from all over occupied Europe.

Wojtyła was a witness of the terror. He saw children removed from their parents and deported. He saw Jews rounded up and sent God knew where. He saw schools, universities, and seminaries closed down. He saw Nazis in jackboots strutting round the city he loved. His father had died in the first year of the war, and he was now, at twenty, an orphan. He joined in the spiritual and cultural resistance movement associated with the Rhapsodic Theater which performed patriotic plays in secret.

He had come to admire the tough resistance of Archbishop Adam Sapieha, and in 1942 joined him in his Palace as a clandestine theological student, though he continued to work for the Solvay chemical factory. Ironies abounded. When Hans Frank called on the cardinal, Sapieha would pointedly invite him to share the corn coffee, beetroot jam, and black bread that were all Poles had to eat. Tucked away in a corner of the Palace was Wojtyła.

Poland was undergoing its "dark night of the soul." It was not surprising that Wojtyła, thanks to the influence of Jan Tyranowski, a tailor and a remarkable lay apostle, should have discovered the Spanish mystical poet, St. John of the Cross. Years later, in his retreat to the Vatican, he quoted the following lines:

To attain to this which you know not
you must pass through that which you know not.
To attain to this which you possess not
you must pass through that which you possess not.
To attain to this which you are not
you must pass through that which you are not.

For Poland the war had been an experience of dispossession, and of discovery.

In their Blitzkrieg against Poland, the Germans brought an entirely new tactic into play. Their armored and motorized striking forces—no longer employed in support of advancing infantry—now operated as independent units.

They made deep breakthroughs into the enemy lines (left). Infantry units followed on trucks, to secure the conquered terrain. Against the mobile tank units, the courageous Polish cavalry (below) was powerless. Back in 1920, after the battle at the Vistula River, they had driven the Russians back 400 kilometers (265 miles) to the east within just a few weeks. But now the Germans had marshaled entire tank units against Poland. It was their striking force and their mobility that made the short, decisive victory—the Blitzkrieg—possible.

WORKER AND STUDENT

Intellectual life in wartime Poland had officially ceased. Universities and seminaries were closed down. In order to survive, Wojtyła had to find work and so be equipped with the precious *Arbeitskarte*. Without it, he was liable to be rounded up and deported to forced labor. He began work in the stone quarry linked with the Solvay chemical works, then a Belgian-owned company (it still exists, but under a different name and different management). In the winter of 1941–1942 he was transferred to the water purification department of the same factory. In his new job he had to carry buckets of lime on a wooden yoke, and mix them with water in just the right proportions. Years later he was to write one of his most moving poems *The Quarry,* which expressed both the dignity and the humiliations of working life. His experiences as a worker left him with an abiding sense that man is made, sculpted, by the work he does:

Hands are the heart's landscape. They split sometimes
like ravines into which an undefined force rolls.
The very same hands that a man only opens
when his palms have had their fill of toil.
Now he sees: because of him others walk in peace.

While at work, Wojtyła continued to study. Small groups were meeting clandestinely to read poetry and perform plays. His interests were still predominantly literary, but now literature had become a form of spiritual resistance. If the Nazis believed that the Poles were fit only for slave labor, then the best riposte was to keep alive the cultural traditions of Poland. Wojtyła had rented a flat in 10 Tyniecka Street from his Wadowice friend, Mieczsław Kotlarczyk, founder of the Rhapsodic Theater.

There had been popes of humble origins before the twentieth century, but they were mostly peasants. John Paul I was the first pope of working-class origins. But John Paul II was the first pope who had himself been an industrial worker. He would never forget the experience.

Old acquaintances, forty years later. Kazimierz Musial and his wife receive the news that the stone quarry worker they knew, Karol Wojtyła, is now pope.

Opposite page: The student. Karol only had one year of normal university study. Then war broke out, and he had to go to work in the Solvay lime-stone quarry and pursue his studies in secret.

Seen posing for this recent photograph (above) are Karol's old comrades Kazimierz Musial and Wicenty Rzycki, surrounded by younger workers in the same plant. Here Wojtyła spent eight hours a day breaking up stones, out of doors even in the bitterest cold. Although he was later transferred to the water purification department, he still had to perform hard physical labor.

He has remained close to his old friends from the quarry and water works. The newly appointed Cardinal Wojtyła gave them a hearty reception in the Kraków Archbishop's Palace (left).

PASSION FOR THE THEATER

The old Rhapsodic Theater in Kraków, founded by Mieczyslaw Kotlarczyk and Karol Wojtyła (both from Wadowice) in 1941, was kept closed by the state censors for many years. Today it is reopened, rechristened the Grotesque Theater, and performs classical and satirical plays. As a theater of the resistance in Poland's worst hours, the Rhapsodic drama group helped to keep alive the hopes and faith of the Polish people.

Top: As early as 1939, Karol and his friends founded a student theater group, "Studio 39." The students wrote, staged, and performed their own plays. This photograph of the young actor Wojtyła is from their poster.

Opposite page: When the Germans overran Poland late in 1939, Studio 39 went underground. Although menaced by the Gestapo, the group remained active until it was transformed, in 1941, into the Rhapsodic Theater. This poster from Studio 39's earliest days presented portraits of the whole company, including Wojtyła (indicated by the arrow, far right).

Wojtyła's passion for the theater, despite the unpromising circumstances of wartime Poland, cannot be exaggerated. With his friend Kotlarczyk he worked hard on "the theater of the spoken word." Since all the conventional resources of decor and scenery were denied them, the living, spoken word had itself to provide the setting and to evoke what was not seen. As Wojtyła wrote after the war (under his pseudonym, Andrzej Jawień): "The word is the key to dramatic ferment —a ferment through which flow the deeds of men and out of which they draw their dynamism."

He had begun acting as a student before the war. At Kraków he had joined the *Studio Dramatyczne* in 1939 which experimented with verse plays on heroic themes from Polish history as well as performing modern plays and cabaret. He acted in a play by Marian Niżynski, *Knight of the Moon*, based on an old Kraków legend. Each of the actors represented a different sign of the Zodiac, and Wojtyła, since he was stocky and tough looking, played the part of Taurus, the bull. At the end of the performance he would take off his bull's headpiece and chase the other actors round the stage. But in wartime Kraków acting was a serious, committed business. It was no time for student japes.

Drama was being used to stiffen the morale of the Polish people. It helped to keep alive the flicker of hope. The plays performed by Kotlarczyk and his troupe were shown before small audiences of fifteen to twenty in private flats, cellars, or the backs of shops. They were full of patriotic sentiments. One of their most popular performances was "Wyspiański's Hour," selections from the works of a nineteenth-century playwright, poet, and painter who had used historical themes to throw light on the sufferings of his own age. The relevance to the 1940s was evident.

Kotlarczyk has recalled the atmosphere of these evenings: "Unforgettable Wednesdays and Saturdays despite terror and arrests. The rehearsals of works by the greatest Polish writers and poets went on, often in a dark, cold kitchen, sometimes with just a candle or two. But we firmly believed in our survival; we were sure we would reach the frontiers of freedom, always faithful to the idea of our theater." It was indeed committed theater, *théâtre engagé*.

udio dramatyczne „39"

oto-Bielec

One evening Wojtyła was reciting the dying words of the priest in Adam Miekiewicz's epic poem, *Pan Tadeusz:*
I fought for Poland: where and how? That story
I shall not tell: 'twas not for earthly glory
That I so often faced the cannon's roar.
I would remember not my deeds of war
But quiet and useful acts, my sufferings
which no one....
At this point in his recital a loudspeaker blared out in the street with an announcement from the German high command of another great victory in Russia. Wojtyła neither stopped nor faltered. He went on reading above the irrelevant noise from the street:
... The night was passing, over the milky sky
The rosy beams of dawn began to fly,
And pouring through the windows on the bed
Like diamond rays about the sick man's head.
It was a straight conflict between poetry and propaganda, two ways of using language, one a corruption and distortion, the other a freeing of language for greater expressiveness. Dawn would come.

Besides acting, reading, and directing plays, Wojtyła also tried his hand at writing them. At least one, *Before the Jeweler's Shop,* has survived. Television companies are now vying for the rights. It is basically a monologue on the sacrament of marriage. Here is a characteristic passage: "Love carries people away like an absolute, though it lacks absolute dimensions. But acting under an illusion, they do not try to connect that love with the Love which has such a dimension. . . . Sometimes human existence seems too short for love."

It should be clear that Wojtyła did not regard acting and the theater as mere aesthetic escapism. In a later article he paid tribute to what he had learned from Kotlarczyk. He stressed the discipline involved in suppressing arbitrary and individualistic styles of acting. For him the actor's business is not to "create" a new and feigned character but rather to "mediate" one who already exists. "The Rhapsodic Theater," he wrote, "required a great subordination of the actor to the dictates of the great poetic word. This became particularly evident when the word expanded in faultlessly spoken choral scenes. A group of people unanimously, as it were, subjected to the poetic word has a sort of ethical significance: solidarity and loyalty to the word." Wojtyła's passion for theater eventually led him out of and beyond it; but he remained grateful for what he had learned there.

THE SEMINARIAN

In 1944 Archbishop Sapieha saved Karol Wojtyła from the Nazis' clutches and hid him in the Archbishop's Palace, where his theological studies went on in secret. Two years earlier, Wojtyła had gone to the archbishop and stated flatly: "I want to be a priest."

The Kraków Archbishop's Palace (right), in Franciscan Street, a stately seventeenth-century building, was the residence of Archbishop Sapieha. Under his protection some thirty seminarians, including Wojtyła, studied here between 1944 and 1946. They lived, slept, and studied in the rooms immediately adjoining Sapieha's private apartment.

In 1942 Wojtyła's studies took a completely different direction. He became a student of theology in the underground seminary run by Archbishop Sapieha, while continuing to work at the Solvay factory. He has never fully explained what made him decide to become a priest. His father's death had moved him deeply, and he prayed for twelve hours by the body. He had had two serious accidents in which he had been close to death. His mystical tailor friend, Tyranowski, was certainly an influence. He may have concluded that with two thousand Polish priests missing or dead, he ought to help to replace them. The fact that spiritual weapons were all that could be opposed to Nazi military might may also have influenced his decision.

The events of 6 August 1944 showed just how dangerous his decision was and left him immured in the Archbishop's Palace until the liberation. What happened was this. A few days after the Warsaw uprising, Gestapo and SS units descended upon Kraków and arrested all males between the ages of fifteen and fifty. There were sounds of shooting in the streets. Wojtyła stayed in his flat in Tyniecka Street and

prayed. The house was not searched. But from this Black Sunday onward, the archbishop decided that the seminarians would live in his Palace and sleep on makeshift beds in the drawing-room; they would not emerge until the Germans had gone.

But having abandoned his work at the Solvay factory, Wojtyła was now without an *Arbeitskarte* and was therefore a non-person. His absence was reported to the authorities. Letters for him began to pile up suspiciously at his old flat. In the end Sapieha intervened and the manager of the factory, a Pole working under German orders, contrived to "lose" his papers so that officially he no longer existed. Meanwhile he was getting top marks in his philosophical and theological studies.

THE YEAR 1945

Kraków was liberated by the Red Army in January 1945. Wojtyła could come out of hiding. Poland had been provided with a Government of National Unity with Władysław Gomułka, one of the leaders of the Moscow-dominated People's Army (AL), as vice-premier and Bolesław Bierut, specially flown in from Moscow, as president. The Home Army (AK), which had taken its orders from the Polish government in exile, refused to recognize this imposed regime, and for two years sporadic fighting continued in which Pole opposed Pole.

Above: Bitter capitulation at the end of the Warsaw uprising. For two months, from 1 August to 2 October 1944, the people of Warsaw had held out against the Germans until the last resistance crumbled. The Soviet army was nearby, unable or unwilling to help. The photograph shows Countess Tarnowska with General von Rohr negotiating the terms of the cease-fire.

The years 1939 to 1945 marked Poland's deepest degradation and also her most heroic resistance. This people accustomed to misfortune lived in the daily experience of terror and death; the misery of imprisonment, hunger, deprivation; homelessness and destruction. At right, signs of the wartime horrors: the notorious death-fence of Auschwitz; a family's attempt to flee, from one terror to another; and the conquered Warsaw.

There were warning signs in Kraków. In 1945 Wojtyła narrowly escaped arrest by the Russians when he was singing Polish patriotic songs in the market square. It is not clear why this should have been an offense. On the other hand, Wojtyła himself recounts the story of a young Russian soldier who appeared at the seminary lodge when he was acting as porter and asked to join. He never did, but they had a long conversation from which Wojtyła concluded that "God can penetrate the minds of men in the most unpromising situations, and in spite of systems and regimes which deny his existence." The

The Warsaw uprising pitted 50,000 Polish resistance fighters, led by General Bor, against the German army. After the capitulation Hitler ordered the complete destruction of the city (left). Surviving resistance fighters were deported to death camps, or slaughtered at once. Throughout the destruction, the Red Army gave no help. Two years later the new Polish Republic was founded under President Bolesław Bierut (below).

incident made a deep impression on him. It convinced him that God could act in unexpected ways, and "write straight on crooked lines."

Much of Poland lay in ruins. The immediate tasks of rebuilding a shattered country and resettling displaced persons were immense. The first Polish post-war government was nominally a coalition which included representatives of the Peasants' Party (SL) led by Mikołajczyk. But in the preparations for the parliamentary elections of January 1947, the Peasants' Party and its supporters were tricked and cheated when they were not arrested and murdered. The result was an unashamed seizure of power. It laid the basis for the Stalinist regime which ruled Poland with a heavy hand until 1956. The scene was set for a confrontation between Church and state which went on, despite partial agreements, throughout the early 1950s. It was not a propitious moment to become a priest. But Wojtyła was ordained on 1 November 1946 by Archbishop Sapieha. Next morning he said his first mass on the feast of All Souls in the chapel of St. Leonard in the cathedral of Wawel.

At the Angelicum, the Dominican seminary at the Church of Saints Dominic and Sixtus in Rome (above and at left), Wojtyła completed his doctoral studies with honors "magna cum laude." He received his highest grades (50 out of 50) in the oral examination and in the defense of his thesis, as the record shows (right).

Karol Wojtyła had to wait until he was twenty-six before he went abroad for the first time. He was sent by Archbishop Sapieha to the Angelicum University, which then as now was in the hands of the Dominicans. The supervisor of his thesis on "The Concept of Faith in St. John of the Cross" was Fr. Réginald Garrigou-Lagrange, who was famous for his rigorous and unabashed Thomism. Wojtyła was given a *summa cum laude* for his thesis, but only parts of it were published in Latin and in Polish. After he became pope, requests to republish the thesis were rejected by a Vatican spokesman, who explained: "We do not wish to see the Holy Father embarrassed by the publication of a text which does not necessarily reflect his present views." This is understandable: no one wants the ghosts of *juvenilia* to return and haunt him in later life. But it would be interesting to know why he now regards it as unsatisfactory: was there too much emphasis on the "negative way" of knowing God?

Among the other professors at the Angelicum during the time Wojtyła was there were Fr. Paul Philippe and Fr. Luigi Ciappi, who later became cardinals and were present at the two conclaves of 1978. They represented extremely conservative attitudes which were not characteristic of the Dominicans in other parts of the world.

During his time in Rome, Wojtyła stayed at the Belgian College. This gave him an opportunity to perfect his French and also to meet people like Fr. Marcel Eulembroek, at that time secretary of the Young Christian Workers movement (Jocistes). He used his vacations to work among Polish refugees in France, Belgium, and Holland and to study the pastoral methods used in these countries. In a letter to Poland he made rather a cryptic comment on what he saw: "Pastoral methods are something which are very difficult to describe and assess. What one can achieve depends on the grace of God and one's own awareness under the grace of God." It would be difficult to apply Western European methods in the circumstances of Communist Poland.

Back in Rome after his summer vacation, he had a sense of "time flying by." Each day was "filled to the brim." But he felt stimulated—and this remained a characteristic—by the demands being made upon him: "My studies, thinking, and meditations all work on me as the spur does on the horse." He does not seem to have had doubts about the methods of

FACULTAS _theologica_

CURSUS ___/___

ANNUS _Laurea_

N.	COGNOMEN	NOMEN	Examen praecipium Dies	Examen praecipium Votum	Dissertatio Votum	Defensio Dis. Dies	Defensio Dis. Votum	Nota
52	Uylenbroeck Mechlinien.	Marcellus						
53	Vachon Quebecen.	Ludovicus			20/20	3-5 '49	19/50	19/... summa
54	Vecchio Lungren.	Franciscus	18-6 '48	41/50				
55	Veseo C.Orat.	Alexander						
56	von Gunten O.P.	Franciscus	3-6 '49	48/50	20/20	15-6 '49	50/50	293/... summa
57	Waldschmidt C.S.C.	Paulus	15-6 '48	45/50	18/20	18-6 '48	48/50	183/2 magna
58	Walgrave O.P.	Valentinus						
59	Wojtyła Cracovien.	Carolus	14-6 '48	50/50	18/20	19-6 '48	50/50	263/2 magna
60	Züger Basilien.	Josephus	14-10 '48	39/50	15/20	23-3 '49	41/50	226/3 cum l.
61	Kenneally C.M.	Guillelmus	1-6 '48	45/50	18/20	2-6 '48	44/50	179/... magna
62	Crépault Quebecen.	Paulus			17/20	9-6 '48	42/50	127/... cum l.
63	Dorris	Rolandus			16/20	9-6 '48	42/50	122/...

teaching then in vogue. In one of his innumerable letters to friends in Poland—clearly he felt the pain of exile—he wrote: "The system under which I am learning is not only tremendously wise, it is also beautiful. And at the same time it speaks with such simplicity. It turns out that Thought and Depth never need many words. Perhaps the deeper the Thought, the less it needs words. It is still difficult to write about my experiences." This text suggests that, whatever his professors may have intended, Wojtyła discovered in St. Thomas Aquinas not so much the system-builder or the crabbed caricature of later scholasticism but the contemplative who described his theological work as "mere straw." It is also worth noting that this approach to the study of theology leads quite naturally into poetry, which Aquinas also wrote.

Wojtyła also became familiar with the sights and sounds of Rome. He was never a systematic tourist, but liked to drop in to churches that were on his way. Later, during the Second Vatican Council, he was to write a poem on St. Peter's called "The Marble Floor." This poem admirably sums up one aspect of his Roman experience, and could in fact be called "prophetic":

Our feet meet the earth in this place;
there are so many walls, so many colonnades,
yet we are not lost. If we find
meaning and oneness,
it is the floor that guides us. It joins the spaces
of this great edifice, and joins
the spaces within us,
who walk aware of our weakness and defeat.

Peter, you are the floor, that others
may walk over you (not knowing
where they go). You guide their steps
so that spaces can be one in their eyes,
and from them thought is born.
You want to serve their feet that pass
as rock serves the hooves of sheep.
The rock is a gigantic temple floor,
the cross a pasture.

47

BETWEEN ACTION AND MYSTICISM

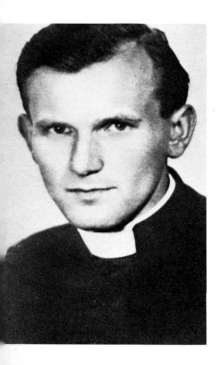

Immediately following Wojtyła's return from his studies in Rome, Cardinal Sapieha sent the young priest (left) to the small village parish of Niegowic, so that he could gain some practical experience in pastoral life. The archbishop transferred him, just a year later, to St. Florian's Church in Kraków.

Right: The house occupied by the vicar of Niegowic was modest, distinguished in no way from the others in the village. In grateful remembrance of his first priestly assignment, Cardinal Wojtyła had a new church built in Niegowic in 1967.

In the Franciscan church just opposite the Archibishop's Palace in Kraków there is a stone memorial to Cardinal Adam Sapieha. He never wore his cardinal's robes. "I shall not wear them," he explained, "so long as my country is suffering." The memorial plaque to Sapieha is inscribed with the words, "Prayer in the Dark Night of Occupation."

It was the Carmelite poet, St. John of the Cross, who had talked of the "dark night of the soul" as the necessary purification which the Christian must undergo if he is to be ready to encounter God. Karol Wojtyła was drawn to John of the Cross and thought at one time that he had a vocation to the Carmelites. But according to Bishop Groblicki, Vicar General of Kraków, he was told, *"Ad maiores res tu es"*—"you are made for greater things." But the Carmelite influence remained, with all its pregnant paradoxes: God is the darkness that illumines, the music that is soundless. In his retreat to the Roman Curia in 1976 he said, quoting John of the Cross: "Man needs mystery for his interior life, for his steady approach to God in the darkness of faith; for although the darkness hides the face of God, it also unveils the infinite majesty of his holiness." His thesis at the Angelicum University in Rome in 1947 was "The Concept of Faith in the Writings of St. John of the Cross."

But if, on his return from Rome in 1948 he still had any lingering nostalgia for the Carmelite life, no one could have suspected it, for he plunged avidly into pastoral and intellectual activity—first of all in the country parish Niegowic and then, a year later, at St. Florian's Church in Kraków. He arrived at St. Florian's carrying only a small suitcase and a packet of books. One of the parishioners asked where his luggage was. "It's here," he said. The people of St. Florian's remember his Franciscan spirit and his battered soutane as much as his spell-binding sermons. The key to his ministry was constant availability. In 1951 he was moved to the parish of St. Catherine's in Kraków. St. Florian's went into mourning. But Wojtyła did not forget them.

OBRAS ESPIRITVALES
que encaminana vna alma ala perfecta vnion con Dios.
Porel Venerable P.F. IVAN DELA CRVZ, primer Defcalzo
dela Reforma de N. Señora del Carmen, Coadjutor de la
Bienauenturada Virgen. S. Terefa de lefus Fundadora de
la mifma Reforma.
Con vna refunta dela vida del Autor, y vnos difcurfos porel P.F. Diego
de lefus Carmelita defcalzo, Prior del Conuento de Toledo.
Dirigido al Iluftrifimo Señor Don Gafpar de Borja Cardenal dela Santa
Iglefia de Roma, del titulo de SANTA CRVZ en Hierufalen.

IMPRESO EN ALCALA POR LA VIVDA DE ANDRES SANCHES
EZPELETA. ANNO DE M. DC. XVIII.

In his theological studies at the university in Kraków, Wojtyła was already fascinated by the figure of the great Spanish mystic, who had reformed the Carmelite religious order in the sixteenth century. For his dissertation on John of the Cross written in Rome in 1947, he was awarded the degree of Doctor of Theology in Kraków in 1951.

Wojtyła's retreat sermon preached before Paul VI and the Roman Curia in 1976 referred to God's infinite majesty and the call to experience it in absolute quiet "like Trappists in their monastery, like Bedouins in the desert, and even like Buddhists." And here he quoted St. John of the Cross as a witness to such mystical experience:

To attain to this which you know not,
you must pass through that which you know not.
To attain to this which you possess not,
you must pass through that which you possess not.
To attain to this which you are not,
you must pass through that which you are not.

Title page of the Spanish edition of the "spiritual works" of the "venerable John of the Cross," in which Wojtyła immersed himself for his doctoral thesis (1947) in Rome, as well as for his own spiritual guidance. A cardinal's coat of arms appeared on the cover of the printed edition of 1618. Wojtyła first became aware of the works of St. John of the Cross at the Carmelite church in Kraków (below).

THE SPORTSMAN PRIEST

On his bicycle Wojtyła often took off into the High Tatra mountains in southern Poland. He is a tough mountain climber, and even as a cardinal he put on his skis every winter. During winters in Rome he sometimes managed to take off for winter sports in the Abruzzis. When asked by a group of Milanese students, in summer 1978, how many Polish cardinals were skiers, Wojtyła replied: "Fifty percent."

Bicycle trips proved useful during the difficult 1950s, when the Stalinists suppressed the

Wojtyła had been keen on sports as a boy. As a young priest, and even as a cardinal, he continued to walk in the mountains, to ride a bike, to ski, and to canoe. As a curate he had led the boys of St. Florian's down by the floodmeadows of the Vistula to play football. His motive was partly to escape from the "cage" of the office and to fill his lungs with good clean air. But it was also apostolic. Since only Communist youth movements were allowed to exist, a hike through the woods was the nearest he could come to a retreat for his students. When out camping he always carried a portable altar so that he could say mass. A cross would be formed by lashing together two paddles. Characteristically he was away canoeing in 1958 when he was named auxiliary bishop of Kraków. Cardinal Wyszyński's staff in Warsaw spent several hours trying to get in touch with him. He was eventually discovered, went to Warsaw to learn the news, accepted, and went back to his canoeing holiday.

Church's work with youth. Groups continued to meet nevertheless in the forests around Kraków. Here Wojtyła would celebrate mass outdoors.

In his contacts with young people, on hikes, and in sports, Wojtyła paid no heed to clerical protocol and matters of dress. As a bishop he still went hiking in shorts and would let his shirttails hang out just like anyone else. Young people were visibly delighted at the natural ease of their "uncle," as Wojtyła was known to his students. Their candid snapshots—for instance, of Wojtyła shaving while on a camping trip—were obviously not subject to his censorship.

Not being afraid of mishap, Wojtyła never bothered to bring along his vestments "just in case." In the summer of 1958, while on a canoeing trip with students, news reached him of his nomination as auxiliary bishop of Kraków. Called immediately to Warsaw for the consecration, he was forced to borrow a cassock. But no sooner were the formalities with Cardinal Wyszyński completed than he rushed off, in civilian clothes again and without a word to anyone, to rejoin the students and his canoe.

AS BISHOP
DURING THE DIFFICULT YEARS

Polish people revel in processions and pilgrimages. They will travel in fervent numbers to their sanctuaries, which are also national monuments —such as Czestochowa, the site of the Black Madonna. A victory over Sweden in the sixteenth century is attributed to her intervention. She was proclaimed "queen of Poland," according to an inscription in the local monastery of Jasna Gora.

Since Poland became a Communist-ruled people's republic, two opposing symbols dominate the country's ideological life. On the one hand, the bust of Lenin, symbolic of the Party. (Bust from Nowa Huta, the city of the "new man.") On the other hand, the cross and flag (right), which stand for the faith and the nation, two elements which for Poles belong together.

When Wojtyła became bishop in 1958 at the age of thirty-eight, he was the youngest member of the Polish hierarchy. It was a period of relative optimism in Church-state relations. In the darkest days of Stalinism over two thousand bishops, priests, and Catholic lay people had been in prison. Cardinal Wyszyński himself was confined to a monastery in eastern Poland. But then Khrushchev's denunciation of the crimes of Stalin at the Twentieth Party Congress meant a break with the past. Hope was in the air. Gomułka, who had himself been in prison, now became the first secretary of the Communist party, and Wyszyński was reinstated. There was talk of "the Polish spring" and a belief that an independent "Polish road to Socialism" could be followed. Philosophers like Adam Schaff and Leszek Kolakowski were hammering out a "revised" version of Marxism which involved a return to the early, more humanistic Marx. These developments affected the complex relationship of Church and state. A wary truce replaced direct confrontation. But though active and crude persecution now ceased, perpetual harassment continued unabated, and it was not easy to be a bishop.

The battle was on for the "soul" of Poland, and there were two versions of Polish history. According to the official ideology, proclaimed in all the media and not very successful-ly inculcated through the educational system, Poland had become a model Socialist country in which the new "Socialist man" was being forged. According to the Church, Poland was a bastion of Christianity and therefore of liberty, strategically placed in the heart of central Europe. Great events like the celebration of ninehundred years of Polish Christianity in 1966 dramatized the two opposing views and made for conflict. There was no doubt where Wojtyła stood on this question. But he accepted that "Socialism" had come to stay in Poland, was rarely unnecessarily provocative, and, until the late 1970s, did not show much interest in politics. Then he began to press for the implementation of the Helsinki declaration on human rights.

Throngs of people join the Polish episcopal hierarchy (right) in a procession honoring Stanislas, patron saint of Poland and of the Kraków archdiocese. The saint's relics are carried in the foreground, followed close behind by Cardinals Wyszyński and Wojtyła. The devout people of Poland became the Church's solid cornerstone during the difficult Stalinist years.

A man of great intellectual curiosity, even though he feels sympathy with the mystics, Karol Wojtyła is given to action but not to restless, fussy activity. His thirst for action draws him toward people. He is eager to help them, by listening, advising, instructing. He has time for everyone, an ear for everyone. His sense of responsibility toward human beings shines through, whether he is addressing the faithful in a sermon (below) or inviting old friends to dinner in the bishop's curia (top right). His friendship also embraces his old

father-confessor Edward Zacher (below left) from the village of Wadowice. He remains available to perform marriages for acquaintances, and in his spontaneous, uncomplicated way signs autographs leaning on a schoolboy's back (pictures below left).

Wojtyła rejoices in dialogue and in conversation, because he is open to the world and to reality. He is not fond of polemics. He prefers to leave politics, such as the negotiation of compromises between Church and state, to Poland's primate, Cardinal Wyszyński (below), the seasoned fighter for Church rights. In his native gifts, his passion, and temperament, Cardinal Wyszyński is a born politician, who has proved to be equally independent of the state and of Vatican policy. It was thanks to Wyszyński that the diocesan boundary disputes in the country's formerly German eastern areas were finally resolved.

NOWA HUTA:
SYMBOL OF RESISTANCE

Groundbreaking, 1967, for the church of Nowa Huta. Ten years later, at the consecration, the archbishop spoke on human rights, such as religious freedom, the right to work, and—in a passage suppressed by the censor—the right to a fair wage. Before that, Wojtyła had come to Nowa Huta year by year to attend a requiem for four-hundred Poles whom the Nazis had murdered in the nearby hills of Krzeslawice. As reminders of such suffering, Polish sculptors have created several versions of the Pietà (below) at the entrance to the crypt.

Traveling eastward from Kraków, you soon come to a bleak redeveloped area. Huge gray concrete blocks jut into the sky. Each bears a big black number, just as each of the apartments inside is numbered. This is Nova Huta, Poland's first "Socialist town," which was planned by the Party to be the birthplace of the "New Man." In thirty years (1948–1978) the population has reached 200,000. The greater part is employed in industry. A prominent feature is the Lenin plant, producing some two million tons of steel a year.

The New Man was to be emancipated from religion, and so there was no room for a church in the drawing-board town. Yet Sunday by Sunday, thousands were soon gathering around a small chapel, out in the open, for devotions. Neither rain nor snow could keep them away. In 1957, after many petitions, the authorities permitted a cross to be set up on this site, already allocated for building. Three years later came the sudden announcement that the space was urgently needed for a school. A team of workmen appeared to remove the cross. This provoked tumultuous resistance: police cars were overturned, many arrests were made.

A determined citizens' committee and an energetic priest eventually obtained permission to build a church. But from the ground-breaking in 1967 till the consecration, another ten years were to elapse. With building machinery not available, the people voluntarily relied on their own hands. Two million stones, which the faithful got from the mountain streams of their home areas, have made the outer walls as live as they are weatherproof.

The church which they enclose is crowded to overflowing twelve times every Sunday. The parish of Nova Huta has itself become a monument to the fact that peasants who have become workmen need not "of historical necessity" lose their faith. And the next generation? Fourteen thousand children have been enrolled in the parish for religious instruction.

"May the visitor make his peace with God, with his fellow man, and with himself." Thus reads, in large letters and in several languages, the message at the entrance to one of the three chapels under the nave of the "Noah's Ark" of Nowa Huta. It is intended also as a sign of reconciliation between Poles and Germans. Groups of the German "Atonement" movement helped with the building, and international Catholic solidarity assisted financially. In the Reconciliation Chapel, a statue by the Polish sculptor Antoni Rzasa (below) commemorates the priest Maximilian Kolbe, the martyr of Christian love, who gave his life for a father imprisoned with him at Auschwitz. The chapels permit services to be held for groups in a more private setting, and the huge gallery above the main church can be partitioned into smaller rooms for lectures or special devotions. On great feasts, as at the celebration of first communion in May, the church interior is opened toward the court. For the construction, the priest had organized a design competition even two years before the government permit was issued. In the design adopted, the architect has developed ideas inspired by Le Corbusier's Pilgrim Church in Ronchamp.

WITH POLAND'S PRIMATE

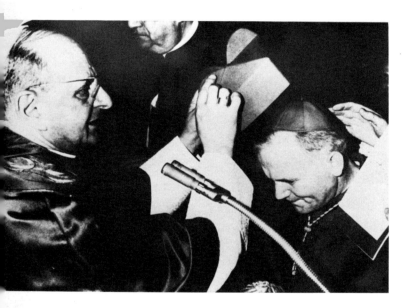

Karol Wojtyła's rise through the Church hierarchy was swift and brilliant. Named auxiliary bishop in 1958, then archbishop and metropolitan of Kraków in 1964, he received from the hands of Pope Paul VI, in 1967, the red hat—or, more properly, the red biretta of the cardinal (left). Thereafter Pope Paul often summoned Wojtyła to participate in congregations of cardinals, which obliged him to travel repeatedly to Rome to attend the plenary sessions.

He shared the honor of being cardinal in Poland with the Warsaw "primate," Cardinal Wyszyński (right). Wyszyński's historical role, like his personality, is without equal in the Catholic Church. His face radiates spiritual refinement and earnest dignity, and photographs of a laughing or even a grinning Wyszyński are rare. The naming of a second Polish cardinal, and then of a third in 1973 (Kominek, who died a year later), has in no way diminished the primate's uniqueness. With the twenty-year difference in their ages, Wyszyński and Wojtyła are "colleagues" who incorporate two distinct generations of Polish Church history. Wyszyński, the fearless defender of the Church's rights against the Stalinists, felt that by being on the scene he knew better than Rome when it was time for resistance and when accommodation was called for. In his first settlement with the People's Democratic state he risked the displeasure of Pope Pius XII, and he never supported the papal Ostpolitik, the official Eastern European policy, of Paul VI. Wojtyła was always loyal to Wyszyński, even though the two differed in temperament and outlook, Wojtyła being close to the Catholic intellectuals of the "Znak" group and having a greater interest than Wyszyński in the new Conciliar movement.

Both at home and abroad, Cardinal Wyszyński had become the symbol for the defiant resistance of the Polish Church. He had seen three first secretaries of the Communist party come and go and could afford to take the long view. His authority was unquestioned. As priest, bishop, and later cardinal, Wojtyła always remained intensely loyal to the primate, who was twenty years older. When Wojtyła was made a cardinal in June 1967, it was suggested that the government would be able to exploit the fact that there were now two Polish cardinals. The churchmen always knew that "divide and conquer" was the obvious tactic to use against them, so they maintained an unbreakable united front. In a letter written shortly after he became pope, and addressed to the Polish people, John Paul II devoted a special section to Cardinal Wyszyński. "My very reverend and beloved primate," he wrote, "allow me to tell you simply what my thoughts are. There would not be a Polish pope in the chair of Peter today, were it not for your faith which did not fear prison and suffering, your heroic hope, your total confidence in the Mother of the Church; were it not for Jasna Góra and that whole period in the history of the Church in our country that has been linked with your ministry as bishop and primate."

"Things eternal, things of God, are very simple and very profound. We don't have to create new programs; we have to find new ways, new energies and a new enthusiasm for sharing in the eternal plan of God, and of fulfilling it in the context of our times. The Council has set things in motion, but for many of us its decrees are as yet merely written documents. I want to awaken the archdiocese of Kraków to the true meaning of the Council, so that we may bring its teaching into our lives."

Words spoken by Karol Wojtyła on the occasion of his consecration as archbishop of Kraków, 8 March 1964.

"We want the climate of truth to become that of our social life. We want to see a true picture of ourselves in newspapers, on the radio, and on television. We do not want an artificially contrived truth, a manipulated public opinion. But what we read and what we hear through the media is not a true picture of ourselves—as if Poland were an atheistic country. All sorts of people have the right to address us by way of radio and television, but the sick can never hear mass being broadcast or televised. We do not want an authority based on police batons."

From a sermon preached by Cardinal Wojtyła, January 1977.

As the quotations on this page demonstrate, the archbishop and cardinal of Kraków did not base his speeches and sermons on beautiful words, but on life and reality. But his earlier experience with words and expression in drama and literature stood him in good stead. Not the least of his skills in this area was the mastery of timing and the use of effective pauses, as the mass media reporters noted, with evident surprise, after his very first address as pope.

Cardinal Wojtyła had been traveling regularly to Rome since the Council started in 1962. After the Council, his growing international reputation meant that he received more and more invitations to travel farther afield. Each of these journeys had several purposes. Not necessarily in order of importance: they gave him a chance to listen and to learn; to lecture and to preach; to make contact with the local hierarchy; and to meet the local Polish communities who still felt close ties with the motherland. They were also an expression of "collegiality in practice."

His first transatlantic journey was in 1969. He went first to Canada as Cardinal Wyszyński's representative and then to the United States, where, as he explained, he represented only himself. He refused to be drawn on political questions, saying that his visit had a purely religious purpose. The highlight in Canada was the twenty-fifth anniversary of the Canadian Polish Congress held on 13 September, and in the United States it was his visit to Orchard Lake Seminary whose 353 students were all of Polish origin. But everywhere he went, he took pains to meet the local bishops and invite them to Poland. Cardinals Krol and Cody later accepted an invitation.

In 1973 he embarked on a much more ambitious journey to Australia for the Eucharistic Congress held in Melbourne. He emphasized the ecumenical importance of the Congress, since, as he remarked, "this is a continent where so many believers in Christ belong to so many different churches." He also seized the opportunity to visit New Zealand, the Philippines, and New Guinea, where he made an excursion into the bush and was happily photographed in the company of feathered and painted warriors.

But his most important foreign journey came in 1976 when he went to the Eucharistic Congress in Philadelphia, an event associated with the two-hundredth anniversary of the Declaration of Independence. Whereas in Melbourne in 1973 he had been accompanied by two Polish bishops, in Philadelphia he led a delegation of eighteen. Though he remained unwilling to speak badly of Poland when abroad, he spoke on this occasion of "a deep hunger for freedom and justice," which was widely interpreted as a critique of the Polish Government. He also gave important lectures at Harvard University and the Catholic University in Washington.

Archbishop Karol Wojtyła traveled abroad a great deal. He is shown (left) in the Vienna airport changing planes on his way to Rome; on visits to America (below left), with nuns in Chicago, which has a large Polish community, and in New York being greeted by a girl in Polish national costume; and in New Guinea (right and below) with children, and surrounded by warriors decked out in feather cosumes.

RECONCILIATION WITH GERMANY

The Polish Church leaders, the primate Cardinal Wyszyński and Cardinal Wojtyła, are greeted on their arrival at the cathedral square in Mainz, West Germany, by Cardinal Volk of Mainz.

Together we were called to God's vineyard,
to do his work long, long ago. We know the value
and the price of each and every human life:
whether it be German or Polish.
We know it, because we have heard this call:
Let us shape our life according to the Gospel.
Let us give the Gospel the shape of our own life—
though the attempt be difficult and awkward.

From the sermon preached by
Archbishop Cardinal Wojtyła, 24 September 1978,
in the Cathedral of Our Lady, Munich.

The primate of Poland, Cardinal Wyszyński, together with Cardinal Karol Wojtyła, visited West Germany from 20 to 25 September 1978. Throughout the visit the future pope avoided the spotlight of publicity. As in Poland, the archbishop of Kraków subordinated himself to the undisputed authority of Wyszyńsky, the primate. He remained the junior partner, although his presence was continually emphasized, both by his German hosts and the Polish visitors, and he played an active part in the events. For at that time Wyszyńsky—seventy-seven years old and not in the best of health—certainly regarded Wojtyła as his successor as primate, and had arranged their roles above all to allow the subsequent pope to express himself. Despite the painstakingly devised protocol, Wyszyński gave him a more than sufficient opportunity to make his opinions known. In this the long delayed, somewhat overdue return visit to Cardinals Döpfer and Höffner, the representatives of the German Bishops' Conference, the primate played the mainly political role, while it fell to Wojtyła to provide the theological and pastoral emphasis.

What was most striking about Wojtyła's speeches and sermons was the extent to which his remarks were directed to the future. Once only did he refer directly to the suffering caused in Poland by her past relations with Germany, in recalling the years from 1939 to 1945 which, as he said, were part of his own experience. Otherwise, he spoke rather of the dignity of Man, and the need to unite in its defense, under differing political systems. He used the examples of Maximilian Kolbe and of Edith Stein, the Carmelite from Cologne, as starting points for his recollections of the past.

In this way he dealt with the difficulties of recent history. The conclusion: between now and the year 2000 the great need is to remodel the face of Europe. Wojtyła tried to build a bridge between East and West, always reiterating, to German and Polish participants alike, that a world without God meant the death of Man and the end of freedom. In the East, as he made clear enough, the attempt is to impose a godless

world from without, through atheism by state decree, whereas in the West there is a less dramatic process of creeping secularization. The task here, for both bishops' conferences, was to consider together how Christ could be brought closer to man again. In retrospect, here and elsewhere, we are now reminded of the pope's appeal in St. Peter's Square, when he took up his office, as he called out: "Open the doors; yes, throw the doors wide for Christ!"

Wyszyński himself decided on what for him was a politically delicate visit, and on its timing. It was long delayed, for his prime consideration was, and is, the security of the Catholic Church in Poland.

Cardinal Wojtyła, however, had already been able to gain some experience of Germany, both at Cardinal Döpfer's invitation, and also when he received an honorary doctorate from the University of Mainz. Already from Kraków,

together with the editors of the Polish Catholic weekly *Tygodnik Powszechny,* he had been encouraging the early signs of reconciliation with the German section of "Pax Christi," the international Catholic peace movement, and with other groups. On this visit, likable and unpretentious as ever, keeping to the issues and avoiding emotion, he took the process further, Never acting obtrusively, he also never played the know-all armchair critic, wise after the event. He remained the Wojtyła one had known in Kraków, always with a slight smile, stooped and somewhat retiring, noncommittal, and always on hand when needed. This manner, that of the "other" Polish cardinal, practiced in Poland from political necessity, and practically recognizable as Wojtyła's personal style, was here not so much a matter of imposed discipline, as of considered judgment.

LEARNING AND POETRY

Despite his intense pastoral activity as a bishop, Wojtyła managed to complete an important work of philosophy, *The Acting Person* (published in Polish in 1969 and, in a revised and enlarged edition, in English in 1979). Inspired by the work of Max Scheler, one of the Catholic disciples of the phenomenologist Edmund Husserl, it is nothing less than an attempt to describe the human being in all its manifold dimensions. The body, the unconscious, the emotions—all have their due place in this impressive synthesis which also opens into ethical and political philosophy in the final chapter on community and participation. As he explains in his preface, the stimulus to write the book came from the feeling that although science had extended the range of human knowledge, it had not deepened our understanding of man as a person:

Having conquered so many secrets of nature,
the conquerer must have his own mysteries ceaselessly
unraveled anew.

For Wojtyła, wonder is the beginning of philosophy:

Man runs the risk of becoming too ordinary for
himself. . . . It was precisely to avoid falling into the rut
of habit that this study was conceived. It was born out
of that wonderment at the human being which initiates
the first cognitive impulse.

Wonder is also at the origin of his poetry. He still had things to say which the abstract language of philosophy could not express.

*A BISHOP'S THOUGHTS ON GIVING
THE SACRAMENT OF CONFIRMATION IN A
MOUNTAIN VILLAGE*

The world is charged with hidden energies
and boldly I call them by name.
No flat words; though ready to leap
they don't hurtle like mountain water on stones
or flash past like trees from sight.

Take a good look at them as you would
watch insects through a windowpane.
And still, and yet – under the word's surface
feel the ground, how firm to your feet.
(This thought is composed of currents,
not of innumerable drops.)

I am a giver, I touch forces that expand the mind;
sometimes the memory of a starless night
is all that remains.

2
Inward-bent, so many they are, they stand in
    slanting files.
A frail flower, it seems, sprouts from the street
to take root in their hearts.

3
In their features I see a field, even and white,
upturned, their temples a slope,
their eyebrows a line below.
The touch of my open hand
senses the trust.

Karol Wojtyła's poems appeared between 1950 and 1966, at first under a pseudonym and later signed only with initials, in two Catholic periodicals published in Kraków. These years correspond to his career as priest and bishop; no further poetry appeared after he became a cardinal in 1967. The magazines published a total of fifty-one short poems by Wojtyła and two longer cycles of several parts each. The last poetry, the cycle "Easter Vigil," appeared in 1966, inspired by the jubilee celebrating the one-thousandth year of Polish Christianity.

The poems reflect certain aspects of his life. The long work published in 1956, "The Quarry," marked the occasion of a

5

We never see spirit – eye mirrors thought;
I meet thought half way and then turn back.
The eye competes with the face,
opening it up, wiping its shadows away.

6

The shape of the face says everything
(where else such expression of being?).
How telling the eyes of a child,
constantly crossing a strange equator
(the earth remains a small atom of thought).

Invisible pressures are trapped in the atmosphere,
yet there is light enough
to approach in this dark.

7

And who is to come?

8

Everything else enclosed in itself:
grass on the crest of the wind,
an apple tree cradled in space
abundant with fruit.
Man meets Him who walks always ahead,
courage their meeting place,
each man a fortress.

Thought is behind it, a thought – not seeing
but choosing. In the map of their wrinkles
is there the will to fight?
Shadow moves over their faces.
An electric field vibrates.

4

Electricity is fact not symbol.
I look through eyelashes into the eyes:
light through a transparent grove.

The surface connects with the hidden plane,
a frontier running untouched by sight;
thoughts rise to the eyes like moths to the pane,
they silently shine in the pupils – deep,
how deep are human deeds.

turn for the better in Church-state relations in Poland and the release from long imprisonment of Cardinal Wyszyński. The work recalls Wojtyła's years as a worker breaking stones in the quarry during the war. Other poems concerned with work themes are "The Car Factory Worker" and "The Armaments Factory Worker," as well as works concerned with a secretary at her typewriter, an actor, and an intellectual. An important theme in the early poems was the Virgin Mary, who inspired a series of poems called "The Mother," including "Her Amazement at Her Only Child."

The poem quoted here, written in 1961, is the work of Bishop Wojtyła before the Council years in Rome. It is no doubt autobiographical, revealing Wojtyła's own feelings on the occasion described. It was followed by a companion piece entitled "Thoughts of a Man Receiving the Sacrament of Confirmation in a Mountain Village," which begins "How am I to be born?"

The poems at times take up a theological or philosophical point, without didactic heaviness, but they are generally more direct in tone—celebrations of feelings that can only be suggested, not captured or fully analyzed, or confessions of wonder or perplexity or faith. The style, basically direct, employs free verse and imaginative metaphors, as in this representative sample.

ACTIVITY IN ROME

The Second Vatican Council (1962–1965) put Wojtyła in direct contact with the worldwide Church and involved him in a major turning point in Church history. As early as the second session, in 1963, he addressed the Council on wording of the Constitution of the Church (Lumen Gentium). On becoming an archbishop, he made a plea on behalf of dialogue between clergy and laymen, as well as between the generations; on this occasion he was interviewed by journalists in Rome (left). His most engrossing concern was the so-called Clause 13 concerning the Church and the world. He addressed a plenary session of the Council on the lack of dialogue:

In the text that we see here, the Church is doing nothing but instructing the world, since she speaks from the treasures of truth that are hers alone....
Clause 13, on the contrary, must so express itself that the world will recognize that we ... are working *together* with the world to seek a true and just solution to the difficult problems of human life. The question is not whether the truth is manifest to us, but rather how the world can find and appropriate the truth to itself. Every teacher knows from experience about what is called the "heuristic method": the student is enabled, so to speak, to find the truth within himself. This method excludes anything that betrays a "clerical" approach: for example, the hue and cry over the alas! lamentable state of the world today ... or the all-too thoughtless appropriation by the Church of all the good that exists in the world ... such attitudes place obstacles in the path of dialogue with the world, from the outset; and so this dialogue remains a monologue, a soliloquy. Let us take care that our Clause 13 not become a monologue!

Wojtyła first came to the attention of the wider world through his attendance at the four sessions of Vatican Council II (1962–1965). He did not conform to the stereotype of the Polish "conservative" bishop. He made important contributions on religious liberty (the Church can only claim as a right what it is also prepared to concede) and on atheism (there should be dialogue rather than condemnation). Subsequently he attended all the Synods which have taken place in Rome between 1967 and 1977. In 1971 he was elected to the permanent Council of the Synod, and he gained an increasing number of votes in later elections: in 1974 he came fourth in the election to the Council. His performance at successive Synods led to a close friendship with Paul VI who had nominated him to several of the Roman Curia's administrative bodies such as the committee for the clergy, liturgy, and education. In 1976 the pope invited him to preach the Lenten retreat for himself and the Curia (later published as *Sign of Contradiction*). Though he may not have been widely known to the public at large, he had become well-known to many of the cardinals who would be present at the conclaves of 1978.

As a delegate to the Council, Wojtyła (shown in a circle in the picture) happened to be seated beside a black African bishop, with whom he became good friends (as mentioned in a poem he wrote at the time). Thus he may have had Africa, as well as Poland, in mind when he discussed the theme of the Church and the world of today, during his address to the second Council session. This theme inspired Wojtyła to criticize the proposed draft of the Lumen Gentium *text:*

It is unavoidable that the *man of today, himself,* be reached. When we speak of the "world," we must not lose sight of the human being—man, who lives in various "worlds," under diverse economic and political systems. He is our concern, he is the subject of our deliberations in this document.

Predecessor and successor. Pope Paul VI, with his successor, Albino Luciani, cardinal of Venice, on a journey through the canals of the city, sometime during the last years of Paul's life. He died on 6 August 1978 at Castelgondolfo. Three weeks later, on 26 August, Luciani was chosen pope and took the name John Paul I.

A short thirty-three days after the election of Albino Luciani, an astonished world learned that John Paul I had died. The conclave, the second convened within seven weeks, caused another surprise in the world with their choice of Karol Wojtyła as pope. It is rare indeed to see the succession of three popes within a single year—but this was not the first time it occurred. One must, however, go back to the sixteenth century to find a pontificate that lasted as briefly as that of John Paul I.

When Cardinal Wojtyła paid homage to Pope John Paul I on the occasion of his election and investiture (right), he had no idea that he himself—as Pope John Paul II—would be receiving this traditional homage of the cardinals, less than two months later. Both Albino Luciani and Karol Wojtyła were named cardinals by Pope Paul VI.

Pope Paul VI died on the evening of 6 August 1978, feast of the Transfiguration. The cardinals in conclave surprised themselves and the waiting world by electing Albino Luciani, patriarch of Venice, within a single day. He took the name of John Paul I as a sign of continuity with both his predecessors. He died on 28 September, after only thirty-three days as pope. The second conclave of the year was a much grimmer affair. There was less confident talk about "God's candidate" and the action of the Holy Spirit. The Italian press spoke about a "strategy of tension" which suggested that in the apocalyptic age we lived in (Aldo Moro's will had been released and rockets were hurtling down on the Christians of the Lebanon) a "strong pope" would be needed to overcome the crisis. The secret of the conclave has not been broken, but the most reliable sources and reasonable inference lead one to conclude that it was the insoluble conflict between two Italian cardinals, Benelli and Siri, which led the 111 cardinals to envisage a non-Italian. On the eventing of 16 October Wojtyła was elected. In answer to the question put in Latin, "Do you accept?" he replied, after an agonizing pause: "With obedience in faith to Christ, my Lord, and with trust in the Mother of Christ and of the Church, I accept."

WHITE SMOKE
FROM THE SISTINE CHAPEL

The conclave is over. The Vatican "housekeeper" checks the lock on the bolted door to the Sistine Chapel. The cardinals, locked in since the evening of 14 October 1978 and protected by members of the Swiss Guard, had the task of choosing the successor to Pope John Paul I.

Two days later their work was done. But the new pope-elect detained them for one more night, so that they could dine together and celebrate mass the next morning. The cardinals lined up (below) as the pope in his new vestments walked out of the chapel. He alone wears a miter, in token of the cardinals' respect. Beside him walks the master of ceremonies.

Though the pope had already been elected, it remained to tell the world. After the confusions of 26 August, when it was not at all clear what color the smoke was meant to be, on 16 October there were fewer doubts. Cardinal Krol of Philadelphia painted a touching picture of the newly elected pope, seated alone at the table before the immense fresco of Michelangelo's Last Judgment, head in hands, body slumped forward. Cardinal Basil Hume of Westminster said: "I felt desperately sad for the man. But somebody had to carry this tremendous burden, and be confined in this small area. There comes a time when all the clapping stops, and when the new pope ceases to be news." But he added that the new pope had the toughness to cope with the situation.

Meanwhile Cardinal Pericle Felici, Latinist and dry canon lawyer, had appeared on the balcony of St. Peter's to tell the waiting world, just as he had done a month before. "We have a pope," he announced amid cheers, "his name is *Carolum. . . .*" This had the vast crowd puzzled. The only "Charles" they could think of was the eighty-five-year-old Cardinal Confa-

lonieri who had undoubtedly played a discreet role in the preconclave proceedings but who surely had not been elected pope, even in this year of surprises. . . . *"Carolum Wojtyła,"* went on Felici, relishing his moment of suspense; but no one was much wiser.

It took time for the truth to sink in, even among the "experts" gathered for radio and television comments in the left-hand *braccio* of St. Peter's Square. The unusual name was not that of an African or an Asian but of a Pole. *Un Polacco.* Outside in the crowd, and especially after his friendly first speech, there was great enthusiasm. "After all," said one man, "the Poles are better Catholics than we Italians." And someone else said: "From now on he's an Italian."

It seemed that all the conventions about conclaves had been broken at once. The conclave had elected the first non-Italian for 455 years. It had, moreover, elected a relatively young pope, the first fifty-year old since Pio Nono. And it had taken the risk of electing someone from a Communist country.

On the evening of 16 October 1978, one hour after the white smoke from the chimney of the Sistine Chapel told the waiting world that a new pope had been chosen, he appeared on the balcony of St. Peter's, before Rome and the world. John Paul II, a Pole, the first non-Italian pope in four and a half centuries, opened his mouth and astonished his audience by addressing them in fluent Italian, starting with the time-honored Catholic greeting: "Sia lodato Gesù Cristo," "Praised be Jesus Christ."

Sia lodato Gesu Cristo! Dear brothers and sisters, we are all still grieving the death of our dearly beloved Pope John Paul the first. And behold, the most eminent monsignors cardinals have called a new bishop of Rome. They have called him from a distant land, far, but yet nearby because of our communion of faith and Christian tradition. I have feared this appointment, but I have accepted in the spirit of obedience to our Lord Jesus Christ and in full confidence in the Holy Madonna. I do not know if I express myself well in your . . . in our Italian language. If I make mistakes, then please correct me. And thus I appear before you to give testimony of our joint faith, of our hope, of our trust in the Mother of Christ and in the Church. And now we follow this road of history and of the Church, with the help of God and the help of all people.

"PRAY FOR ME, SO THAT I CAN SERVE YOU"

Standing beneath the "harrowing of hell" in Michelangelo's painting The Last Judgment, *John Paul II celebrates with the cardinals his first mass as pope, in the Sistine Chapel, on the morning of 17 October 1978.*

The first major address of John Paul II was delivered the morning after his election while the cardinals were still, officially, in conclave. Yet he spoke to a wider audience: "to the cardinals, to the sons and daughters of the Church, and to all people of good will." The new pope did not present a program for his pontificate, and declared his conviction that the future course of the Church could not be predicted in advance. "What is the fate," he asked, "that the Lord has in store for his Church in the coming years? And what path will humanity take as it draws near to the year 2000? These are difficult questions to which we can only reply: God knows." Then he asked for the prayers of the whole Church to enable him to fulfill his mission.

Further excerpts from the pope's address in conclave, 17 October 1978:

There is one section of the Vatican Council to which greater attention will have to be given, and that is the ecclesiological section. Venerable Brethren and beloved sons of the Catholic world, we have to take once more into our hands the *Magna Carta* of the Council, that is the dogmatic constitution *Lumen Gentium,* so that with renewed and invigorating zeal we may meditate on the nature and function of the Church, its ways of being and acting. This should be done not merely in order that the vital communion in Christ of all who believe and hope in him should be accomplished, but also in order to contribute to bringing about a fuller and closer unity of the whole human family.
John XXIII was accustomed to repeat the following words: "The Church of Christ is the light of that nation." For the Church—his words were repeated by

the Council—is the universal sacrament of salvation and unity for the human race.

*   *   *

Nor must we forget the Brethren of other Churches and Christian confessions. For the cause of ecumenism is so lofty and such a sensitive issue that we may not keep silent about it. How often do we meditate together on the last wish of Christ who asked the Father for the gift of unity for the disciples. Who does not remember how much St. Paul stressed the "unity of the spirit" from which the followers of Christ might have the same love, being "of one accord, of one Mind"? Therefore one can hardly credit that a deplorable division still exists among Christians. This is a cause of embarrassment and perhaps a scandal to others. And so we wish to proceed along the way that has been so happily opened up, and to encourage whatever can serve to remove the obstacles, since we desire that through common effort full communion may eventually be achieved.

*   *   *

And that is the reason why our address must yield to prayer. And after our prayer to God, we feel the need for more prayer to plead for the necessary help, which is to enable us to continue the work of our predecessors. After having remembered the latter with emotion, we are grateful to extend greetings to each one of you most reverend cardinals.

JOY IN POLAND

If the election of John Paul II, the first non-Italian pope for 455 years, was greeted with pleasure throughout the world, in Poland itself it stirred deeper emotions. Poles were incredulous, overjoyed, moved to tears. It was as though some of the humiliations that had been heaped on the country throughout its troubled history were now lifted.

In Warsaw that same evening, Mr. Kazimierz Kakol, minister of religious affairs, had been holding a press conference for visiting journalists. He stressed the importance for Poland of the conclave. Its outcome would determine whether the *Ostpolitik* of the Vatican, which under Paul VI had been seeking a cautious accommodation with the Communist countries, would be continued or not. "And if," he added, "a Polish pope were elected"—general laughter greeted this preposterous suggestion—"I will buy you all champagne." Half an hour later, Kakol, pale but faithful to his word, ordered champagne. The Polish government was torn between its politics and its patriotism. It chose patriotism and sent a telegram of congratulation. In Warsaw church bells rang out, and hardly anyone went to bed.

But down in Kraków, the feeling of joy was accompanied by a deep sense of loss. A student said: "He was our friend, but now he has gone to be a friend of the whole world." A woman on the tram said: "He has gone from us, but he will stay in our hearts." On the day after the election a vast crowd gathered in the square outside the cathedral of Wawel. Only a few weeks before, on 28 September, Cardinal Wojtyła had said mass on the twentieth anniversary of his episcopal ordination: it was the last time he had been seen in public in Kraków before setting off for the fateful conclave. But now the crowd assembled spontaneously. There had been no announcement of a mass. Word of mouth was enough to fill the square. As the mass came to an end, the thousands began to sing the hymn that is sung each morning at Czestochowa as the Black Madonna is unveiled. There were more tears.

In Kraków the independent Catholic weekly Tygodnik Powszechny *confirmed the incredible radio reports. Issues of the paper soon fetched black market prices.*

78

HABEMUS PAPAM!
JAN PAWEŁ II
Jerzy Turowicz telefonuje z Rzymu

SIGNS AND SYMBOLS
OF THE GREAT OFFICE

The investiture of Pope John Paul II. As Bishop of Rome he received the pallium, a stole worn by Metropolitan bishops (below left). He was already accustomed to the miter (center), worn by all bishops and cardinals, a much lighter headdress than the triple papal crown that now sits in the Vatican Museum, no longer worn by the popes. Fully vested, the pope received homage from the cardinals, among them Poland's Cardinal Wyszyński (opposite page). Then he gave his inaugural address (below right), quoted on pages 84–85.

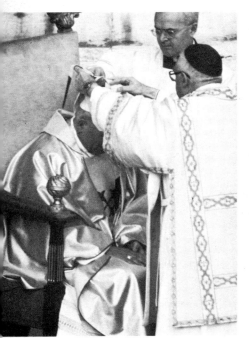  

In his brief pontificate Pope John Paul I had abandoned certain customs and set precedents which John Paul II willingly followed. They were all intended to make the point that the pope was a pastor rather than a sovereign. Instead of the traditional "coronation" with the tiara or triple crown, he preferred to "inaugurate his pastoral ministry" with a mass in St. Peter's Square. The trappings of temporal power—the tiara was an oriental symbol of monarchy—were replaced by an eminently Christian symbol: the conferring of the pallium. The pallium has been presented to metropolitan bishops, of both East and West, since the fourth century: therefore it has ecumenical importance, especially for the orthodox. It is made of lamb's wool, and so signifies pastoral care. It is placed over the shoulders and resembles a yoke: it is a reminder that the service of unity will not be easy. And it is presented to the pope as coming "from the tomb of St. Peter": it therefore emphasizes that all stewardship in the Church is linked with the founding apostle.

John Paul I had also tried to abondon the *sedia gestatoria,* the portable chair on which popes had been traditionally carried aloft through the crowds. He did not use it at his inauguration. But he was persuaded to use it again within three weeks of his election, when the Roman crowds complained that they could not see the pope. John Paul II, however, abandoned it definitively. Audiences, meanwhile, had proved too big for the new audience hall, then too big for St. Peter's itself, and in the spring were finally moved outside into the piazza. The pope made sure he was visible by riding round in an open jeep.

81

THE CEREMONY
IN ST. PETER'S SQUARE

On a mild autumn morning, at ten o'clock, John Paul II inaugurated his ministry as supreme pastor. Red and white gladioli surrounded the altar. The crowd was estimated at over 300,000. The Polish delegation of over 2,000 was headed by the president, Henryk Jablonski. The embrace for Cardinal Wyszyński was particularly prolonged and emotional. At the end of the ceremony, John Paul II again ignored protocol and went down to greet personally the Poles who had come to Rome for the mass. That same afternoon he received the visiting ecumenical delegations, and stressed the "irreversible" nature—thumping out the word—of the Church's commitment to ecumenism. He invited all those present to link hands as a pledge of their unity in Christ.

The inauguration mass celebrated outdoors on 22 October 1978 before some 300,000, including President Henryk Jablonski of Poland and the Polish minister for religious affairs. Afterwards the new pope called to the audience, in Italian: "It is time to go and eat—for you and for the pope!"

The absolute and yet gentle power of the Lord corresponds to the whole depths of the human person, to his loftiest aspirations of intellect, will, and heart. It does not speak the language of force, but expresses itself in charity and truth. . . . Open wide the doors for Christ. To his saving power open the boundaries of states, economic and political systems, the vast fields of culture, civilization, and development. Do not be afraid. Christ knows "what is in man." He alone knows it.

John Paul then said a few words in Polish. They were (we are told by Poles) a marvel of expressiveness. Something comes through even in translation:

What shall I say to you who have come from my Kraków, from the see of St. Stanislaw, of whom I was the unworthy successor for fourteen years? What shall I say? Everything that I could say would fade into insignificance compared with what my heart feels, and your hearts feel, at this moment. So let us leave aside words. Let there remain just great silence before God, the silence that becomes prayer. I ask you: be with me at Jasna Góra and everywhere.

Even the most garrulous commentators had nothing more to say.

*   *   *

But before this stirring conclusion, the inauguration sermon had offered several important passages that are worth quoting here:

To the See of Peter there succeeds today a Bishop who is a son of Poland. But from this moment he too becomes a Roman. Yes—a Roman. He is a Roman also because he is the son of a nation whose history, from its first dawning, and whose thousand-year-old traditions are marked by a living, strong, unbroken,

Pope John Paul II began his homily at his inauguration mass in Italian before breaking into other languages toward the end. By quoting the most famous novel of Henryk Sienkiewicz, *Quo Vadis,* he hinted at his reluctance to accept the office of pope and at the same time his readiness to accept what was the will of the Lord. Peter was leaving Rome during the persecution of Nero and met Christ along the road. "*Quo vadis,* where are you going, Lord?", he asked. Christ answered: "I am going to Rome to be crucified again." Crestfallen, Peter returned to Rome to take the place of Christ. Paul VI had used the same story, and given it a melancholy, resigned ring. But there was nothing tremulous in John Paul's recounting of it.

In the central passage of his homily, he developed the Christian humanism that flows from his philosophy and issued a ringing challenge to the whole world:

The words quoted here are from the pope's inauguration homily, delivered before the microphones and television cameras of half the world (including Poland) and to the huge crowd (photograph on next pages) that jammed the spacious Renaissance square.

and deeply felt link with the See of Peter, a nation which has ever remained faithful to this See of Rome. Inscrutable is the design of Divine Providence.

*   *   *

Our time calls us, urges us, obliges us to gaze on the Lord and to immerse ourselves in humble and devout meditation on the mystery of the supreme power of Christ himself. He who was born of the Virgin Mary, the carpenter's son (as he was thought to be), the Son of the Living God (confessed by Peter), came to make us all "a kingdom of priests."

The second Vatican Council has reminded us of this power and the fact that Christ's mission as a priest, as a prophet, as a king, continues within the Church. All of God's people share in this threefold mission. Perhaps in the past the triple crown was placed upon the head of the pope to express by this symbol God's plan with his Church, namely that the whole hierarchy of the Church and all of the sacred power exercised by her is no more than a service: the participation of all God's people in this triple mission of Christ, and the resolute loyalty of these people to submit always to God's will, which does not trace its origin to wordly power, but to the mystery of the cross and the resurrection.

The absolute and yet sweet and gentle power of the Lord responds to the whole depths of the human person, to his loftiest aspirations of intellect, will, and heart. It does not speak the language of force, but expresses itself in charity and truth. The new successor of Peter in the See of Rome today makes a fervent, humble, and trusting prayer: Christ, make me become and remain the servant of your unique power, the servant of your sweet power, the servant of your power that knows no eventide. Make me be a servant, indeed, the servant of your servants.

Brothers and sisters, do not be afraid to welcome Christ and accept his power. Help the pope and all those who wish to serve Christ's power to serve the human person and the whole of mankind. Open wide the doors for Christ. To his saving power open the boundaries of States, economic and political systems, the vast fields of culture, civilization, and development. Do not be afraid. Christ knows "what is in man." He alone knows it.

So often today man does not know what is within him, in the depths of his mind and heart. So often he is uncertain about the meaning of his life on this earth. He is assailed by doubt, a doubt which turns into despair. We ask you, therefore, we beg you with humility and trust, let Christ speak to man. He alone has words of life, yes, of eternal life.

*   *   *

I open my heart to all my Brothers of the Christian Churches and Communities, and I greet in particular you who are here present, in anticipation of our coming personal meeting; but for the moment I express to you my sincere appreciation for your having wished to attend this solemn ceremony. And I also appeal to all men—to every man—and with what veneration the apostle of Christ must utter this word: "Man."

Pray for me.

Help me to be able to serve you! Amen.

"I STILL HAVE TO LEARN TO BEHAVE LIKE A POPE"

Right from the start, John Paul II made it clear that his pontificate would be different in style and that he would imprint upon it his own strong personality. He had a way with crowds, and showed a disregard for protocol which visibly distressed his master of ceremonies. Within two days of his election he had committed himself, without any hedging reservations, to Vatican II, to collegiality and to ecumenism. He had also emerged from the Vatican to visit Polish-born Bishop André-Marie Deskur who was in the Gemelli Hospital. He traveled in an open car and was cheered along the route. Despite the problems created for the security forces, he would not be content to remain "the prisoner of the Vatican." Later he would make a point of trying to visit a Rome parish every Sunday, often staying with the clergy and people until 9 or 10 in the evening. Since he was now Bishop of Rome, and since this was the foundation of all his other titles, he would try to be a bishop who was close to the people, just as he had been in Kraków.

But wider international responsibilities were not neglected. On 18 October he addressed the diplomats accredited to the Holy See. There were no apologies or confessions of inexperience in his speech. It was as though he had been waiting to say these things for years. He was anxious to underplay his "Polishness" and said that "from now on the particular nature of our country of origin is of little importance." He added: "As a Christian, and still more as pope, we are and will be witnesses of a universal love." But his Polish experience colored his plea to the nations for justice so that Christians "may be able to nourish their faith, be able to worship God as they will and, as loyal citizens, play a full part in the social life of their countries." This was a discreet foreshadowing of the theme of human rights which became a constant of his papacy.

At home with diplomats, he was equally at ease with journalists at his first meeting with them. He did not have the fund of anecdotes of his predecessor, but after his speech he moved down the Hall of Benedictions exchanging greetings and fielding multilingual questions with skill and good humor. Asked how he felt after five days in the Vatican, he said that he found life there "tolerable." Pressed to say whether he would go here or there, he replied that he would "if *they* will let me." Meanwhile the members of the Roman Curia wondered how they would fare in the new regime. In the event they were retained in their old posts, but did not start a new term of office. In other words, John Paul II kept his hands free for the future.

But the most striking first impression—subsequently confirmed—was of the man himself and his extraordinary success with crowds. The broad, slightly hunched shoulders, and the face that conveys a sense of strength and conviction, became known the whole world over. His voice is firm and clear. He has the habit of emphasizing certain key words as though punching them irrevocably home. ("With what reverence the apostle of Christ pronounces the word 'man'.") Unlike his immediate predecessor, whose thirty-three-day pontificate had been a whirlwind rush, John Paul II never gave the impression of being in a hurry. Though he was no less active and energetic, and wrote speeches at great speed, he seemed to take his time, as though pacing himself for a long pontificate.

At the same time, it was evident that John Paul II was still learning how to be pope. He kept on forgetting to give his blessing at the end of audiences, and had to be reminded of this by the by now somewhat frantic master of ceremonies, Mgr. Virgilio Noè. He also worried the Vatican tailors, Gammarelli, who were disturbed to see no shirt-cuff visible beneath the sleeves of his white soutane: they hastened to provide him with twelve shirts and a set of cuff links. There are stories of him, in his early days, getting lost in the Vatican, and suddenly appearing in remote offices. Then he got his Irish secretary, Fr. John Magee, to show him around, and he no longer makes mistakes. After lunch he sets off on a brisk two-mile walk round the Vatican gardens, accompanied only by his Polish secretary, Stanislaw Dziwisz, who used to ski with him in Poland: no one else can keep up with them. "I don't work any harder than I did in Kraków," he told a Polish friend, "the only strain is that in Kraków I worked mainly in Polish. Here I am constantly switching languages."

The numbers coming to public audiences grew and grew. The pope's habit of plunging into the crowd whenever he felt like it gave his security men nightmares. At one audience he found an eight-year-old boy who was weeping. John Paul II stopped to ask him why he was crying. "My father died three days ago," said the boy, "but they told me that you, too, were my father. Is that true?"

"Certainly it is," said the pope, hugging the child, "and you may call on me as you would on your father." He told an usher to get the boy's name and address. It will not be the last time he meets the pope.

The popularity of the Polish pope became something of an embarrassment. In the spring of 1979 audiences moved into St. Peter's Square itself, and over eight hundred coaches blocked the approaches. Frustrated motorists grew angry and hooted. It was suggested that audiences should take place in the afternoon rather than in the morning, to ease the crush. It was also proposed that the coaches be parked on the Janicu-lum Hill and called down by radio by the police as they were needed. The Italian Embassy to the Holy See spent much of its time in coping with the security arrangements, involving over a thousand men, which were needed every time the pope emerged for one of his visits to the parishes of Rome. The Rome Tourist Council, however, did not mind in the least: they calculated that John Paul II had attracted over five mil-lion tourists in the first six months of his pontificate, and in gratitude they gave him a gold model of the Colosseum.

That he should have had a twenty-five-meter swimming-pool specially built at Castelgandolfo shocked some while delighting others: it seems that this pope has a genuine need to work off surplus energy that is not met by brisk walks in his garden. The Curia, meanwhile, was feeling neglected: the pope was spending his time with the crowds in St. Peter's Square and not paying sufficient attention to his bureaucracy. But he told a Polish friend that he intended to be his own master. "They told my predecessor," he said, "what he should do and when, and this may have led to his early death. They will not tell me what to do or when. I will decide. They will

Since the days of Pius XII (far right), the style of the Vatican has been transformed. Pope Pius (1939–1958) still wore the bejeweled tiara with its three crowns, which evoked the temporal, feudal claims of the medieval papacy. Accompanied by the Byzantine-style plumed fan (right), he was carried aloft on his throne or sedia. John XXIII and Paul VI gradually dispensed with such pomp. John Paul I declined any kind of crown.

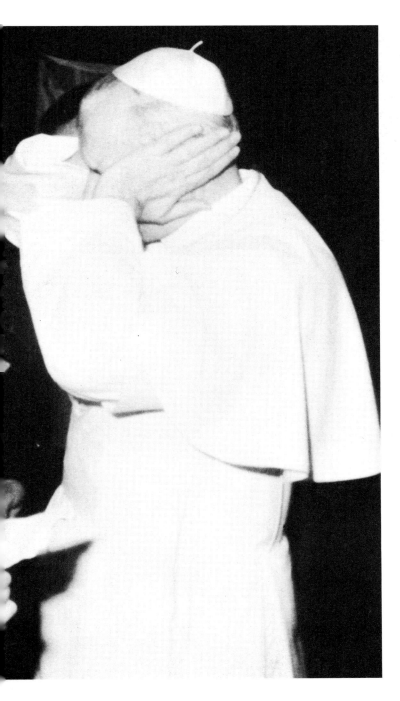

not kill me." One of his major innovations in the Curia is to ask to see the authors of draft documents rather than work only through the heads of their departments. In May he made his most significant appointments. Archbishop Agostino Casaroli became acting Secretary of State, while the Spanish-born diplomat Archbishop Eduardo Martinez Somalo was made his deputy or *sostituto*. Commentators noted the return of the *sostituto* to a subordinate role (it had become a position of great power in the pontificate of Paul VI), the confidence shown in Casaroli (who was not without his critics in Poland), and the way the new pope did not feel the need to appoint collaborators who would "balance" each other. In other words, as he planned his Polish trip, he felt confidently in command of the Roman Curia. He was learning fast.

PILGRIMAGE TO THE MADONNA
OF GUADALUPE

At the goal of his pilgrimage to the Virgin of Guadalupe: Pope John Paul addresses the faithful from the cathedral balcony.

John Paul II made his first major journey as a pilgrim. Both of the predecessors whose name he bears, John XXIII and Paul VI, had also made pilgrimages of their own. Before the opening of the Second Vatican Council, Pope John traveled to Loreto and Assisi: a short journey, but even so the first break in the boundaries that the papacy had drawn round itself in the last hundred years. Pope Paul's pilgrimage was a biblically motivated "return to the origins," to the land St. Peter had left nineteen hundred years before, to the holy places of Jerusalem. The Polish pope was making a different kind of pilgrimage. Ever since his childhood, like so many of his countrymen, he had venerated the "Black Madonna" in the sacred painting at the national shrine of Czestochowa. Now, as pope, he would bring the same devotion to the Madonna in her non-European figuration. Although he felt the call of the whole continent, the actual invitation came from Mexico. For the pope, however, the sanctuary of Guadalupe was the goal of the journey, and in this he went right to the heart of the Mexican people, for whom this place is the best loved in

the whole country. A carpet of flowers before the pilgrim church showed how the people had anticipated the pope's own feelings; it read: "Mexico and Poland United in Love of Mary."

Was this no more than a happy coincidence to open the festivities? One might almost suppose so. But behind it stand certain coincidental parallels in the histories of the two countries. Just as the Poles see in the image of their Black Madonna at Jasna Gora the symbol of their originality, their powers of resistance, and their religious loyalty, so too is the sacred Madonna of Guadalupe the embodiment of what we might call the "identity" of the Mexican people. In this case it is not the identity of a people repeatedly partitioned and threatened like the Poles, but rather a people deprived of their entire cultural heritage, and wounded to the core of their dignity by colonial overlords. Indeed, the Madonna of Guadalupe represents the first recognition by Christianity of the Indians and thus—throughout Mexico—the beginning of their conversion. For, according to tradition, it was in December 1531, ten years after the Spanish conquest of the Aztec empire, that the Indian Juan Diego received a vision of the Madonna. She appeared as a woman of his own people, and spoke to Diego not in the language of the foreign conquerors, but in his own. She offered her love and protection to "all who dwell here on earth," and asked that a church be built so she might stay near the people.

Set against the exclusive claim to authority which till then had linked the Spanish conquerors with "their" Christianity, this message represented subversion. The colonial bishop of Mexico, to whom Diego brought the news, took no notice of the Indian, and was only convinced after a whole series of miraculous occurences. The dwelling of the holy "Mother of God" became a place of refuge for the Indians, and a shrine for the "new people," the Mestizos. Three hundred years later the Mexicans fought for their independence under the priest Hidalgo and the banner of the Madonna of Guadalupe. And even today the same image unites the "Chicanos," the Mexican agricultural workers in California, fighting in Cesar Chavez's trade union for work and a just wage. For ultimately, everyone who discerns in the people's religion a concealed

The sacred painting of Guadalupe. According to tradition, the Mother of God appeared to the Indian Juan Diego in 1531. She appeared on the sacred mountain of Tepeyacac in the guise of a woman of the people, addressing him in his Nua- hatl language. The legend states that her image imprinted itself on his cape. The pope, in his sermon, spoke directly to Our Lady. A portion of his prayer is quoted below.

The Mexican revolt against Spanish rule began in 1810 with the raising of the flag of the Vir- gin of Guadalupe by Father Miguel Hidalgo y Costilla. Even after independence, this flag remained a national symbol, and it continues to exert a profound spell today. The wings of the angel, beneath the Virgin's pic- ture, are colored green, white, and red, which later became the colors of the Mexican national flag.

resistance to the imposition of a foreign culture, sees in the holy image of Guadalupe both a secret "baptism" into the old culture and religion wiped out by the Spaniards, and a sign of hope for the independent achievement of a further step toward the "acculturation" of Christianity so often advocat- ed by far-sighted missionaries. Would the pope take specific account of the Indians in confronting this issue? Would he bring with him a charter for a form of evangelization, and community structure, which would let this people discover the Gospel as if it were a treasure unearthed in their own land?

This people, who in their fervor
call you "La Morenita,"
this people, and with them
this whole gigantic continent,
live in a spiritual unity
thanks to the fact that you are their Mother,
a mother whose love acts
and sustains, and gives her sons and daughters
the chance, time and again, to draw
nearer one another and to God.

REJOICING IN MEXICO

to see his own reflection. In the capital, however, he was shielded from that direct contact with the people which is the witness of the pope's great love for them, by no less than 27,000 security men, some uniformed, some in civilian and even clerical dress. These people were quite ready to make use of truncheons and tear gas to keep the cathedral entrance clear.

Inside the magnificent baroque building, those who had managed to get in defended their minute standing—and

"I welcome you to Mexico, sir": officially speaking, Jose Lopez Portillo, as president, was at the airport to receive a *Señor* from Rome. He was prevented from going beyond this by the constitution of the Federal State, whose anticlerical origins are brought to every tourist's attention by the huge fresco on the staircase of the government palace. But it was before this very palace, on the Plaza de la Constitucion, also know as Zocalo, that the whole nation gathered to welcome their distinguished visitor. According to the proper usage, Lopez Portillo had given him "into the hands of the hierarchy and the congregation of your church": and behold; a million hands reached out to the pope, just during the drive to the city. The police estimated that a total of about 18.8 million Mexicans were on the move during the seven-day visit, to see the pope and to receive his blessing—itself constitutionally illegal in public.

The enthusiasm was easily predictable, days and weeks in advance. Flags and posters with the pope's picture were displayed throughout the land, so much so that someone remarked acidly that wherever the pope looked he was bound

breathing—space against each other. Each of the parishes of this city of 14 million had issued tickets to five members of the congregation, but there were obviously many others who had got in on the strength of their connections. A good few had to content themselves with the sight of the pope on the small television screens suspended from the pillars. At first his address failed to arouse great interest. The theme of the *"virgo fidelis"*— the loyalty of the Virgin Mary—seemed somewhat lacking in topicality. Jubilation broke out only when the pope drew the parallel between the loyalty of Poland and the loyalty of Mexico—*Polonia semper fidelis* and *Mexico semper fidelio*. Then it was "Long live the pope!"

In his address the pope was obviously also trying to preserve the balance within the Church between conservatives and progressives. Only in very general terms did he refer to the persecution and contempt that can result from loyalty to the Church. What was lacking before such a gathering of bejeweled and decorated ladies and gentlemen, clearly occupying privileged positions even here in the Church, was a word of solidarity with the neglected, an allusion to the ever widening

In a special open bus (opposite page) the pope travels through waving and cheering crowds from the airport to the cathedral of Mexico City. "Welcome to the Pope" (left) was emblazoned everywhere, and proprietors were officially ordered to check the condition of every balcony. Even long waits failed to daunt the cheering and cheerful spectators (below).

gulf between rich and poor. There was no mention of actual injustices, and none of the genuine persecution of Christians even then going on in nearby San Salvador, which became public knowledge through a bloody attack on a young people's evangelization gathering.

Disappointment at the pope's silence, on the part of those who had hoped for something more, continued for the next two or three days, but was in no way noticeable among the people at large.

It was clear, also among the most intelligent young people, that what mattered most to them was not what the pope had to say, but that he was there. "He has come to Mexico, and this is the greatest day of our lives," said a shoeshiner from Mexico City who had traveled for eight and a half hours by bus to see the pope in Oaxaca, together with his parents. A taxi driver, though, did speak of a real "*revolucion.*" He could still remember the anticlericalism of the past, and he spelled out the people for whom the pope's visit really mattered: "He loves the poor, the workers and the *campesinos,* the sick and the children, and that is how he has conquered Mexico!"

95

MEXICO: PROGRAM OF THE POPE'S VISIT

DOMINICAN REPUBLIC

SANTO DOMINGO
25 January

1:30 p.m. Landing
The pope kisses the earth of Latin America. Enthusiastic reception by the crowds.
3:45 p.m. First meeting with the bishops, priests, and members of religious orders before entering the cathedral.
5:00 p.m. Concelebration of Mass with the bishops in Independence Square before some 300,000 people.
8:00 p.m. Visit with members of the diplomatic corps.

26 January

Early morning. After Mass in the cathedral, visit to a "barrio" or slum quarter in the capital.

MEXICO

MEXICO CITY
26 January

12:50 p.m. Arrival. Festive ringing of bells in all the churches of the country. Greeting by Cardinal José Salazar, president of the National Bishops Conference. High Mass.
3:15 p.m. Visit with members of diplomatic corps in the apostolic delegation headquarters.
6:45–8:00 p.m. Private meeting with the president of the Republic, Lopez Portillo.

27 January

9:00 a.m. Reception of members of a Polish community in Mexico City.
9:30 a.m. Travel in open bus to Guadalupe.

GUADALUPE
27 January

12:30 p.m. Concelebration of Mass with the bishops from all parts of Latin America.
Official opening of the Bishops Conference.

28 January

Early morning. Departure for Puebla. Stops in San Martin Texmelcan and San Miguel Xoytly. Reception by a worker.

PUEBLA
28 January

12:00 noon Ringing of bells of 300 churches signals the pope's arrival.
1:30 p.m. Open-air Mass before enormous crowds, followed by an ecumenical meeting.
5:00 p.m. Beginning of the Latin American Bishops Conference. Important policy speech.

MEXICO CITY
29 January

8:30 a.m. Visit to a children's hospital.
10:30 a.m. Departure by air for Oaxaca.

OAXACA
29 January

11:15 a.m. Arrival and greeting by natives assembled from the whole region, dressed in folk costumes. Flight by helicopter to Cuilapan.

CUILAPAN 29 January	12:00 noon Greeting by one Indian boy in the name of more than 100,000 natives. 1:00 p.m. Return flight to Oaxaca.
OAXACA 29 January	3:00 p.m. Visit to the small seminary. 4:00 p.m. High Mass with more than 200,000 faithful. Ten Indians consecrated as deacons. 6:30 p.m. Return flight to Mexico City.
MEXICO CITY 29 January 30 January	7:30 p.m. Audience for the representatives of the national Catholic associations. 8:00 p.m. Visit to Miguel Angel Catholic school, and speech on Christian education and youth work. 9:15 a.m. Flight to Guadalajara.
GUADALAJARA 30 January	10:30 a.m. Greeting by the archbishop. Appearances in the Santa Cecilia section of town and before massive crowds in the Jalisco Stadium: confirmation of solidarity with the workers' situation. 11:30 a.m. Speech to a gathering of nuns. 3:00 p.m. "Angelus" on the balcony of the bishop's residence. 4:00 p.m. High mass in the atrium of the Basilica of Our Beloved Lady of Zapopan. Late afternoon. Meeting with the country's seminary students, followed by return flight to Mexico City.
MEXICO CITY 31 January	7:00 a.m. Mass in the Chapel of the Apostolic Delegation. 8:00 a.m. Reception by government representatives from five Central American countries. 9:45 a.m. Meeting with 100,000 students. 11:00 a.m. Farewell audience with journalists. 3:45 p.m. Flight to Monterrey.
MONTERREY 31 January	5:10 p.m. Welcome by Archbishop José del Iesús Tirado Pedraza. Blessing of the population of the city. Return flight to Rome with a stop at Nassau (Bahamas).

BAHAMAS

NASSAU 31 January 1 February	Evening Greeting by state authorities and the people. 1:30 a.m. Continuation of flight for Rome.

ROME

1 February	Greeting by Italian President Giulio Andreotti. Speech by Pope John Paul.

A straightforward listing of the times and dates of the pope's itinerary, so crowded with journeys, events, and meetings, gives an idea of the physical and mental exertion of the Latin American visit. The world followed every gesture and every word of the pope's with rapt attention, and reacted with approval, criticism, and often with concern.

Immediately upon arriving on Latin American soil, he surprised everyone with a gesture that was criticized by many as too effusive: he kissed the ground. And thus the visit began—an uninterrupted series of greetings and receptions, rides in airplane, bus, helicopter, meetings with government representatives (above left: welcoming by the chief of state of the Domi-

nican Republic), with campesinos, industrial workers, students, nuns, priests, and bishops. He constantly faced gigantic crowds whom the marshals could hardly restrain at times (middle picture).

The holy father was not afraid to don an elaborate Indian headdress (above right), to the crowd's delight. Even during liturgical rituals, he did not hesitate to greet—again and again— the people who wanted so eagerly to see him. As often as time permitted, he celebrated mass with the people (opposite page: in Oaxaca).

GUADALUPE
AND THE EVANGELIZATION OF
LATIN AMERICA

In the square facing the new cement pilgrimage church and the old Baroque basilica of Guadalupe, a huge crowd came together to await the pope and the bishops. Beneath the richly decorated portal (right) John Paul greets the enthusiastic Mexicans, many of whom had come from far away to expeience this moment.

From Puebla de Los Angeles, an industrial city ninety miles from Mexico City, three hundred delegates from all over Latin America came to Guadalupe for the festive opening of the Bishops Conference on Saturday, 27 January 1979. A message spelled out in flowers above the portal of the old pilgrimage church announced the theme of the meeting: *"re-evangelización,"* a renewed evangelization of the peoples of Latin America. The pope, for whom this opening session was the official reason for his journey to Mexico, stressed the same theme in his speech to the delegates. He recalled the first bishops and missionaries, who had started this evangelization of an entire continent—this "unique process," "uninterrupted since 1492." Five hundred years later this continent embraces "almost half of the entire Catholic Church," which now is "rooted in the culture of the Latin American people, an essential element of their own identity."

Those in the audience who knew a little history found it odd, in this connection, that the pope made not the slightest reference to the burden of violence, repression, and imperialism that accompanied the "preaching of the joyous gospel message" in colonial times. The robust "pope from Poland"—unlike Paul VI—felt no need to apologize in any way, admitted no responsibility. Nor did he recall, even in passing, the more than eight hundred priests and nuns (not to mention the active laymen) persecuted during the last ten years for evangelizing among the poor—driven out of Latin American countries, arrested, tortured, or killed as martyrs to love of their fellow-man. He did not mention them that evening, either, when he spoke to two special gatherings, a meeting of priests and a group of nuns. On the contrary, he warned against excessively one-sided social commitment, against favoring the poor out of motives that stem "not from the Gospel but from socio-political considerations." His audience, who were in this case all Mexicans, had little need for such warnings: the majority of Mexico's priests and bishops have so far shown no interest in social commitment.

An evangelization of
liberation—*evangelización liberadora*—
has two elements:
Liberation from all slavery,
from personal and social guilt,
from whatever tears apart
men and society.
And liberation allowing
for growth, for becoming more,
toward complete community
with God and men—which can only
come about when God
is all in all, and when no more
tears are shed.

Pope John Paul II in Mexico

PUEBLA: THE LATIN AMERICAN BISHOPS' CONFERENCE

"De-politicization of the Church": To judge from the reports in the mass media, this was a major concern of the pope during his visit to the Bishops' Conference in Puebla. All those persons who associated their piety with the undisturbed possession of their worldly goods, and who saw the Church as a guarantor of law and order in keeping with the present balance of power, had cause for rejoicing. But the second half of the speech was not entirely in keeping with this idea; here the pope raised such eminently political issues as the preservation of human rights and the consideration of the "social costs of private property." The pope, who later, in his journey to Poland, behaved far from "apolitically," could not possibly believe that he alone among the clergy and the hierarchy of the Church was entitled to play a political role.

But just what is meant by "political" and "apolitical"? Every biblical prophecy was political—insofar as such "words of God" concerned themselves with concrete events, with history. The liberation songs of North America's black slaves were also political—though we have since minimized them as "Negro spirituals." And in fact we must apply the "political" label to everything in the way of liberating action, and the theological interpretation and inspiration of such action, that has come about in Latin Amrica over the last decade in the context of the so-called Christian grassroots communities (the *comunitades eclesiales de base*).

It is political in that the "powerless," who had no voice before, are beginning to talk together and to raise hopes that are not only projected into the afterlife. Their hope, like that of all witnesses and martyrs, is founded on the knowledge that the ruling power collapses when people will no longer bow to it.

For a long, long time, indeed, the Church in Latin America did not just bow to the ruling power, but was intimately involved in this power. It was not until the Second Vatican Council, called together by Pope John XXIII, that a sizable group of bishops became aware of this situation. Among them, one man, Helder-Camâra, archbishop of Recife in northeastern Brazil, came to the forefront as the advocate of a "Church of the poor." It was he, together with a group of experts and like-minded bishops, who brought about that

upheaval in the Latin American Church which took shape in the great continental Bishops' Conference of Medellín in Colombia in 1968. Their motto was "liberation," which corresponded to what the experts considered to be the dual dependency of the Latin American people on injust social and international structures, which at the Medellín conference

The archbishop of Recife, Helder Pessoa Camâra, among his people in Brazil's impoverished northeast. He is convinced that the Church must be born "from within the people," with "the Holy Spirit as midwife." In a private audience with John Paul II, he received support for his thesis: "It is not enough to work for the people: we must work with the people." This is the principle of the grassroots communities and consciousness-raising developed by Paolo Freire, an idea put into practice in Recife earlier than anywhere else.

were referred to as "sinful." Liberation presupposes as a starting point that people become aware—be made aware—of this situation. Such a process was spearheaded quite early, for example, in Recife, Brazil, according to the methods of Paolo Freire, who combined literacy classes for poor country people with grassroots consciousness-raising and solidarity groups on a trade-union model. This method, by now world-famous, "lets the teacher die" and respects the integrity of the pupil, who becomes articulate in his fight for survival. But in Brazil the method is called subversive. When a military regime came to power in a putsch, Freire had to leave the country at once. This occurred in 1964, the key year which initiated the highest Brazilian military circles' propagandizing for the "geopolitical" theory of "national security." According to this theory, the entire continent of Latin America, like in fact the whole world, must be considered in a permanent state of war because of the threat of Communism. Whence all other values must be subordinated to that of "national security": and the Church too must be involved in this struggle. The theory developed into a totalitarian ideology, which in turn came to be associated with the practice of torture. This totalitarian trend was already apparent by the time the conference of Brazilian bishops began at Medellín. By now, ten years later, nearly every democracy in Latin America had "died"; the "national security" ideology had spread from country to country and had become the pattern for younger and older military dictatorships alike. These regimes summarily declared elementary human rights invalid—such as the right of *campesinos* (farm laborers and tenant farmers) to cooperative and trade-unionist alliance. In recent years more and more bishops, often at considerable risk, have supported the cause of these workers and the rights of the threatened Indians; but there of course remain the timid souls and those who—in the old tradition of "throne and altar"—stand arm in arm with the reigning military.

Whole conferences of bishops (for example in Brazil, Chile, Guatemala, Panama, and Paraguay) had made their voices heard. On the other hand, at Medellín, the bishops' delegation of Colombia—the host country itself—had refused to sign. And yet Bogotá, in Colombia, was the headquarters of the Bishops' Council for all of Latin America (CELAM). The secretary responsible for the organization of the Puebla Conference, Lopéz Trujillo, was likewise from Colombia. The two-year preparations for the conference were co-managed by Roman cardinal Baggio, whom Paul VI had named first chairman of the meeting. People spoke of the "Rome – Bogotà axis"—meaning the "soft-pedalers." The associate chairman of the conference, however, was the Brazilian cardinal Aloiso Lorscheider. This man, who shared the attitudes of Helder-Camâra and was supported by Cardinal Arns (of Sao Paolo), offered a counterbalance in Puebla to the pope's rather abstract speeches. It is time, he said, to take Latin America's concrete situation into account and to heed the *"grito"*—the "cry of our people." Lorscheider later voiced his disappointment that the Puebla conference had been the scene of "pressures" and "mistrust" and that there had been too little "plenum"—open discussion and general consciousness-raising. The Conference's resolutions worked out in twenty-two committees—a whole book—were unanimously adopted at the end. Despite a good many compromises, the resolutions go beyond Medellín and the papal speeches on at least two major points: They repeatedly stress the importance of the grassroots communities and condemn the "idolization of the state" due to "national security."

HUMAN DIGNITY
AND HUMAN RIGHTS

In the face of an ever more alarming situation, seldom improving, but frequently worsening, the pope wishes to be your voice; the voice of all those who cannot speak, or who are kept silent; the voice of conscience, the call to action, so that wasted time, time often of prolonged suffering and hope deceived, can be made up!

With these words, on 29 January 1978, John Paul II addressed himself to the Indians and *campesinos* who had streamed into Oaxaca, in southern Mexico, and through them to the "great mass of the agricultural population which dominates South America." He made the connection with the great day, ten years ago, when the papacy, through the presence and in the words of Paul VI, proclaimed its "solidarity" with the concerns of the oppressed who worked on the land. This proclamation found an echo across the whole continent, and was, for example, recalled in his last sermon by the priest and martyr of El Salvador, the Jesuit Rutilio Grande, who sacrificed himself for the *campesinos*. But the pope was also

responding to the moving words addressed to him by a forty-eight-year old Indian called Estebán, father of seven children. Estebán, himself a member of the Zapotek tribe and speaking only their dialect, spoke in the name of the native population of Cuilapa, and of the 350,000 Indians from 30 tribes who are often unable even to communicate with each other. He said:

We are a downtrodden people. We suffer much. Our cattle have a better life than we do. We cannot express ourselves: we must contain our suffering in the depths of our hearts. We have no work and no one to help us. But we gladly offer you the use of our little strength. We offer you the church; yours and ours. Holy Father, plead the cause of your poor children with the Holy Ghost. Through my words the people of this country ask for your prayers, that the word of God may become the reality of our lives.

The offer contained in these words is only comprehensible when one knows something of the role of the *Delegados de la palabra,* the "spreaders of the word," in the grassroots communities of Middle and South America today. The words provoked a visible response. The pope undertook a consecration of ten Indians, whom he designated as "lay persons, who should retain that status," to permanent office in the Church as had been the custom in the early Church, before the clericalization of the Middle Ages reduced these offices to no more than the lowest steps toward the priesthood. Even so, this process did nothing to fulfill the hope that a way might be opened for Indians to run their own communities and to celebrate the Eucharist—in other words, to achieve the priesthood—through an entirely different process of instruction, related to their own culture and way of life, and without the obligation to celibacy which they find incomprehensible. This demand, supported among others by the Brazilian bishops (including Cardinal Lorscheider), obviously in the interests of the Indian missions, sadly stimulated no response for the time being, either at Puebla or, seemingly, from the pope.

Nevertheless, the pope spoke the words quoted at the beginning in the context of a "universal request to the Church" to open itself to the evangelization of all races and cultures: "If the Church will offer unrestricted loyalty to the Gospel of the Lord, she must accept the whole reality of Mankind, readily and with understanding!"

"You are the voice of those who are silent" were the words on the floral arch before the entrance to the town of Oaxaca. Indeed, the words of John Paul II in Oaxaca (and also before the industrial workers in the huge stadium of Monterrey) had taken on a new, more urgent tone, in which blatant injustice was called by its true name and the shock of its impact found expression:

The oppressed *campesino,* the worker on the land, whose despair is watered by his own sweat, can do no more than hope that his dignity, which is in no way inferior to that of any other level of society, will receive full and lasting recognition. He has the right to be heard. He has the right not to be deprived of his minimal possessions, by means that are sometimes genuinely degrading. He has the right to strive independently for a life he knows to be better. He has the right to the removal of all the barriers caused by his exploitation.... He has the right to effective assistance, which is neither alms-giving nor a mere gesture of justice. Rather, it must give him that opportunity for self-realization which he deserves on the grounds of his dignity as a human being and child of God.

The pope then advocated "rapid and enduring action, bold and revolutionary innovations, and urgent reforms" in the interest of the communal good, including where necessary the "expropriation" of private property.

The conscience of the people, the cry of the helpless, and above all the voice of God reiterate with me: It is not right, it is not worthy of man, and it is not Christian to preserve conditions which are quite clearly unjust.

"It is not right, it is not worthy of man, and it is not Christian to preserve conditions which are quite clearly unjust." With these words the pope called to mind all those who are disenfranchised and exploited—the human beings condemned to misery. The picture shows a slum in Rio de Janeiro.

"EVERY
SINGLE HUMAN BEING"

Just how much did the pope see in Mexico of the concrete situation of the poor, of their misery in their cardboard shanty houses, and of the desperation of those deprived of even this form of shelter? The question is justified, in view of the marathon program of his journey. At least, he came close enough to one group of the population—the industrial workers—to be reminded of his own "firsthand experiences" during the "difficult years of the World War": "Experiences of the daily grind and all it involved in the way of hardship and monotony."

He said:

I have shared the misfortunes of the workers, their just demands and their legitimate grievances. I know very well how necessary it is for a person to have work that is not alienating and frustrating, to have work that recognizes his full dignity.

Then the pope spoke at length about workers' rights and the significance of the workers' movement:

He who has the good fortune to be able to work, strives for more human and more stable working conditions. Where pay, safety, and the possibility of his intellectual and cultural development are concerned, he will strive also for a fairer division of the fruits of the common effort. Workers want to be treated as free and responsible persons; they want to share in making the decisions that concern their life and their future. They have a fundamental right to form organizations in all liberty for the defense and encouragement of the common good.

Although John Paul's speech was particularly explosive in the context of the workers' rights to organize (rights which are suppressed in many countries of Latin America), on the other hand his words took their place in that series of papal statements which, since the famous letter of Leo XIII (1891), *Rerum Novarum,* on the "labor question," have been known

as "social encyclicals." The last two are entitled *Pacem in Terris* (John XXIII, 1963) and *Populorum Progressio* (Paul VI, 1967).

The pope from Poland also published an encyclical in the very first half-year of his pontificate. It is said that he had already composed it in rough draft during his first five weeks as pope, writing this document "straight from the heart."

It is rightly called a *social* encyclical? Not to outward appearances. Its opening words refer to Christ, savior of mankind: *Redemptor hominis.* The occasion for this encyclical is the pope's entry upon his office. The theme, in any event, is the human being as he encounters, and is encountered by, Christ. Twice in the course of this encyclical we come across the bold sentence from the Second Vatican Council which states that "the son of God in His incarnation united Himself with every human being." The pope stressed this idea still further:

We are concerned with the human being in all his reality, in all his dimensions. We are not speaking of an abstract person, but rather of the real, concrete, and historical person. We refer to every *single* human being; for everyone is involved in the mystery of the redemption, and by this miracle Christ is joined forever with everyone.... Just as man is desired by God, chosen by Him from eternity, called and singled out for grace and salvation, so too is everyone fully "concrete," fully "real." This is the human being in the full light of the miracle in which Christ involves him, the mystery in which every single one of the four billion human beings living on our planet plays a part.

The pope's preoccupation, over many years, with the ethics of the *person* has led him to this conviction of the value of every *single* human being, a belief that is also the foundation of the General Declaration on Human Rights. We see a reminder of this preoccupation in a sentence such as the following: "The exclusive subject of responsibility is the human being himself." It is, above all, the second half of this encyclical that takes up prominent social problems (extending even to the plundering and pollution of the environment), and here it becomes clear to what extent human rights have validity "not alone according to the letter, but according to the spirit." This is the standard for deciding whether every government truly serves the well-being of its people.

POLAND:
PILGRIMAGE OR POLITICS?

Outward harmony between Church and state, June 1979. The flowery "Biedermeier" drawing room in the Belvedere Palace, Warsaw, was the setting for the official talks between Pope John Paul and Polish Party Chief Edward Gierek (seated, middle). President Henryk Jabłonski and Cardinal Stefan Wyszyński are also shown in this cordial moment for official Church-state relations in Poland. But Wyszyński's shadow, seen at center, serves as a reminder of the difficult period of the Polish Church and prompts the question: What lies ahead?

Pope John Paul arrived at Warsaw's military airport in an Alitalia plane at 10:07 A.M. on 2 June. As a visiting "head of stete," he was met by the president of Poland, Henryk Jab-łonski. The Vatican "national anthem"—"traditional" only in the sense that it dates back to Pope Pius XII—was played: it is long, lugubrious, and musically trivial. Polish and visiting bishops were there in force. "You have brought Italian weather with you" was the favorite joke as the sun beat fiercely down. The pope was then driven to Warsaw in an open bus similar to the one he had used in Mexico. Along the route well-disciplined crowds sang hymns as they waited. The previous Sunday sermons had urged everyone to behave with dignity and decorum. Public order was in the hands of the ten thousand volunteer marshals organized by the Church—an unprecedented event in a Communist country. The Church, in other words, was placed on its honor. Police and military were thus enabled to stay in the background, discreetly. They were not needed. The pope was greeted with dignified enthu-

The sacred icon of the Black Madonna of Czestochowa, in the Poles' national shrine, could serve as the dominant symbol of the more religious aspects of the pope's pilgrimage to his homeland. This religious painting has played a great inspirational role in Polish patriotism, even in the country's darkest moments, ever since it was installed in the monastery of Jasna Gora ("Bright Mountain") at Czestochowa in 1382. The Black Madonna came to symbolize the country's resistance to domination by the Swedes and other powers, and was therefore declared, by King Jan Kasimierz, as "Queen of Poland's Monarchs." The icon, of Byelorussian-Byzantine origin, was damaged in the fifteenth century in a Hussite attack on the monastery.

A mute manifestation of the union between religious and patriotic feeling: Poland's national arms (the white eagle) have been combined with a second shield showing the Madonna of Czestochowa.

A great altar erected in Warsaw's large Victory Square bears the names of the Polish saints and blessed, from the early missionary, St. Adalbert, up to Maximilian Kolbe (killed at Auschwitz). Here the pope told the crowds: "Without Christ there could be no history of Poland." The picture of the Black Madonna behind the altar is attached to the huge wooden cross especially mounted for this occasion.

siasm and flowers were strewn along his path.

At two o'clock in the afternoon he arrived at the Belvedere Palace, official residence of the Polish president, for an exchange of gifts and greetings with Mr. Edward Gierek, first secretary of the Polish United Workers' Party (in effect the Communist Party). The two delegations—the pope's suite in black sountanes, Gierek's men in sober suits and ties—faced each other beneath the chandeliers. In his speech of welcome, Mr. Gierek treated the pope rather as if he were no more than

107

The "state visit" began with a reception at the airport. The pope is shown (right) greeted by President Jabłonski. Behind them at left, looking to the side, stands Poland's primate, Cardinal Wyszyński. In his ride through the city of Warsaw in an open vehicle, John Paul was shielded by government security guards from the enthusiasm of the throng.

the leader of an activist movement for peace who could be expected to condemn such frightful horrors as the neutron bomb. He also stressed "the alliance of friendship and cooperation with the Soviet Union" and hoped that the pope would rejoice with him in "thirty-five years of socialism in Poland." The pope's reply was both courteous and subtle. He pointedly made no mention of the thirty-fifth anniversary of socialism, and instead congratulated Mr. Gierek on having rebuilt the Royal Castel in Warsaw, "as a symbol of Polish sovereignty." He spoke of the right of every nation to "political self-determination" and denounced "neo-colonialism" whether economic or military; and there were few Poles—the encounter went out on PK1, the main television network—who did not think of the Soviet Union. Then the pope characteristically forgot to present his gift of a mosaic, and had to be urged

back to the microphone by Monsignor Virgilio Noè, his traveling master of ceremonies.

So much for protocol. Then the visit really began to get underway at four o'clock in the afternoon under a sweltering sun when Mass was celebrated before a huge and orderly congregation in Victory Square, just opposite the tomb of the unknown soldier. The pope's sermon lasted, with interruptions, fifty minutes. It was halted altogether for ten minutes when he said: "Christ cannot be kept out of the history of man in any part of the globe. . . . The exclusion of Christ from the history of man is an act against man." In a country where atheism is taught from the nursery school to the university, this was explosive. Applause rippled across the crowd. Then they broke out into spontaneous song. And finally there were rhythmic chants of "We want God, we want God," just like

football slogans. Victory Square had seen nothing like this before. The pope listened, patiently, his head inclined to the left, and did nothing to encourage or to discourage the display of popular feeling.

As soon as the Mass was over, workmen began to remove the raised dais on which the altar had been set and to dismantle the huge, plain cross, with its flapping red stole, which had dominated the square. It was as though they were trying to erase as swiftly as possible all trace of the remarkable events. But they stayed obstinately in the memory.

Christ is at the center.
Christ cannot be kept out
of the history of man in any part
of the globe....The exclusion
of Christ from the history of man
is an act against man.

The goal of the papal pilgrimage: the monastery and pilgrim church at Czestochowa. The number on the tower shows that Poland already looks ahead to the Madonna's sixhundredth anniversary (in 1982). Banners and signs honor Mary, "Mother of Jesus" (as for example at far right). At the base of the tower one sees the pope's coat of arms (with "M" and a cross) inscribed with his motto "Wholly Yours" in token of his total devotion to Our Lady. He was joined on the podium by the Polish bishops (above), including at far right his successor as archbishop of Kraków, Cardinal-Elect Macharski.

After Warsaw, the pope's pilgrimage took him to the hallowed places closely linked with the origins of Polish faith and national consciousness. He went first to Gniezno, the earliest capital of Poland, and then to Czestochowa, to the shrine of Our Lady at Jasna Gora (the "Bright Mountain"). The Black Madonna of Czestochowa sums up so much of

110

From Silesia—a mining region that the pope was not allowed to visit—came costumed envoys to present him with the gift of a lantern and greetings from their countrymen. The costumes feature hats with feathers from Silesian doves. The region is a rather troubled one, with frequent outbursts of worker dissatisfaction. Since it was a work day, very few Silesians could make the trip to Czestochowa. The procession at Jasna Gora included an elaborately gilded banner of the Black Madonna (right).

Polish history. In 1655 a handful of Polish soldiers and monks successfully resisted a Swedish Protestant army of several thousand men. The following year, in thanksgiving, King Jan Kasimierz dedicated the country to Our Lady, Queen of Poland, and vowed to work for justice among the Polish people. During the period of partition in the nineteenth century, shrines such as Jasna Gora provided a focus for suppressed national feeling, an oasis where, it was said, "Our Lady speaks Polish." Pope John Paul had been to Czestochowa many times before, frequently preaching on the feast of Our Lady, Queen of Poland, on 3 May.

In his sermons during his visit, Pope John Paul, while fully accepting and glorying in his Polishness, kept inviting his listeners to raise their eyes to a wider vision. "Is it not Christ's will," he asked, completely ignoring frontiers and different social systems, "that this Polish pope, this Slav pope, should at this precise moment manifest the spiritual unity of Christian Europe?" He answered his own question thunderingly: "Yes, it is Christ's will." His eye caught a banner in the crowd which proclaimed: "HOLY FATHER, DO NOT FORGET ABOUT THE CHILDREN OF CZECHOSLOVAKIA." The pope read it out in Czech and said, "We cannot forget these brothers of ours," adding—a phrase that was not in his prepared text—"We trust that they can hear us." He was referring to the TV coverage of his visit. The principal Polish channel can be picked up in Czechoslovakia, Lithuania, and East Germany

The pope faces the crowds. Many, like this nun (right) could see his face only through field glasses. Although watching on television would have been more comfortable, many thousands preferred, as the pope said, to "pray with their feet."

(DDR). In fact his appeal was not heard in those countries, except indirectly.

It was in Czestochowa, the most Marian and Polish of shrines, that the pope pledged himself to ecumenism, as though he wished to avert all danger of one-sidedness. He said that he would work for unity and promised "to meet in a more mature way our brothers in faith who are united with us in so many things, though there is still something that divides us." He also had a word for non-Christian religions and "those who are seeking God and wishing to serve him." But despite his deliberate attempts to universalize his message, the visit to Czestochowa marked the moment when the pope really began to feel at home among his own people and to let his heart speak. The Jasna Gora monastery, standing on a hill outside Czestochowa, provides a magnificent and dramatic backcloth: before it stretches a vast field dotted with trees. There was informality and humor as the pope introduced some of the visiting bishops to the crowd. "Poles and Hungarians," he said, introducing Cardinal Lekai of Hungary, "are the best of friends so long as they are drinking together or fighting." And he apologized for forgetting others who who were hidden away "under white umbrellas, seeking the shade." He was visibly moved by the spontaneous singing, and joined in an impromptu folk-singing session. There were tears in his eyes. And everywhere there were children to be blessed and embraced.

Miners dressed in traditional caps and helmets carried flags representing their region or parish.

These commentators from Radio Vatican protected themselves as best they could from the sun, while thousands of worshippers knelt in the huge field (left).

113

AUSCHWITZ: HORROR AND RECONCILIATION

Left: *The cell of Maximilian Kolbe at Auschwitz. This Polish priest gave his life to save the father of a family chosen for execution in a collective punishment. In his prayers at this site, the pope also recalled the carmelite sister and philosopher Edith Stein who was murdered here because of her Jewish family background. Wojtyła had studied the writings of her teacher, Edmund Husserl, and was also, like Edith Stein, interested in the Carmelite order.*

The railroad tracks (at left) that led so many persons to their death at Auschwitz. Thousands of Poles joined the pope here on 7 June 1979 in ceremonies of remembrance and prayers for reconciliation. The deathly railway tracks were strewn with flowers on this occasion.

Thurdsay 7 June was a day of sharp contrasts for John Paul II. In the morning he went home to his native town of Wadowice, where he found the church and his old home repainted in his honor; and in the afternoon he prayed at the site of the concentration camp of Auschwitz where countless numbers of human beings perished. If the atmosphere in Wadowice was that of a carnival, with much greeting of old friends, Auschwitz is a place that chills the heart and makes one wonder, in disbelief at man's inhumanity to man. Despite the constant attention of television cameras and press photographers, Pope John Paul seemed totally lost in prayer as he knelt before the infamous death-wall and the cell where the Blessed Maximilian Kolbe had spent his last famished days. The Mass he celebrated at four o'clock, just outside the barbed wire fence, with the neat rows of once overcrowded huts as backdrop, was the most moving event of the visit so far. Two former inmates were dressed in the striped prison garb and looked plumper than they must have been thirty-five years before. The priests who concelebrated with the pope had all been in concentration camps. One of them

clutched the battered breviary that had been his only consolation in this windswept, desolate place. The crucifix on the altar was surrounded by barbed wire, thus linking the sufferings of Auschwitz with the passion of Christ.

In the pope's homily, compassion and forgiveness overcame all bitterness. He spoke very personally of what the knowledge of Auschwitz had meant for him as a young man: it had convinced him that an ideology which could lead to such horrors must be crazy and, conversely, that he ought to dedicate himself "to the dignity of man, to the threat to man, to his inalienable rights that can so easily be trampled upon and annihilated." There is only a thin and precarious crust between the barbarism that ignores man's dignity and civilization which respects it.

There were more particular messages. The pope wept openly as he spoke of the Jews—one in four of the inhabitants of Kraków before the war was Jewish—who "had received the commandment, thou shalt not kill, and who had experienced to the full what is meant by killing." He mentioned the memorial to the Russian victims of the Nazis, and expressed

his gratitude to the Russian people for the role they had played in the war (a remark that the government eagerly seized upon). And finally he spoke of the six million Poles who had died during the war and the occupation: it had been another stage in their centuries-old struggle for fundamental human rights. If there was a political message here, it was not uppermost in the Pope's mind: the paradox of Auschwitz is that without forgiveness and reconciliation we are all lost.

KRAKÓW:
HOME AT LAST

The residents of his hometown of Wadowice greeted their famous son with many flowers.

Services were celebrated inside churches and out. The pope is seen here in the Kraków cathedral (right). Outdorrs, near the end of his visit, in a mass in honor of St. Stanislas, the crowd is said to have reached two million (picture, overleaf).

The Catholic University at Lublin, where Pope John Paul had once taught, was another place stricken from his itinerary, and so a group of students (below) traveled the 500 kilometers to Kraków. At a particularly enthusiastic moment they all took out the crosses they had been concealing and held them up toward the pope. Tears were shed, but by evening the mood was more jubilant.

On arrival in Kraków, the city with which he had been identified for so many years, John Paul II went to the Archbishop's Residence in Franciszkanska Street. The nuns had been preparing the place all day, sweeping and scouring. There was the first hint of unpleasantness from the police when the students gathered outside the residence and sang songs to entertain the pope. They had always regarded him as their friend and had called him familiarly "uncle" (*wujek*, diminutive of *wuj*). The pope understood perfectly well why they were there, even if the police did not, and at midnight he told them to go to bed, "otherwise you will fall asleep during my sermon tomorrow." They laughed and went home. Kraków is not a very big city, and throughout his stay the pope was never very far from people, many of whom he recognized. Extra meetings were fitted into his crowded program: he met the intellectuals of *Znak,* a Catholic weekly magazine, over breakfast, told them that he admired their work, but that the *samizdat* or underground press was even

more admirable. The government had denied him permission to got to Nowa Huta, where he had consecrated the magnificent new church on 15 May 1977, so instead he went to Moglia where there is a smaller church. He grasped the chance to speak about work and its intrinsic dignity. "The pope," he said, "has no fear of the workers—they have always been particularly close to him." He then denounced the view that "man should be considered merely as a means of production," which could be taken as a critique of both state capitalism (as practiced in Communist countries) and *laisser-faire* capitalism. The tall steel mill chimneys of Nowa Huta were visible in the background as he spoke.

The visit was drawing rapidly to a close. Throughout the night of 9–10 June pilgrims slept in the churches of Kraków while the students sang their songs in the main square, gathered round the statue of Adam Mickiewicz. They were preparing for the Mass on Sunday morning celebrated in Blonie, the vast flood meadows alongside the Vistula River which offer a unique panorama of the city of Kraków. There were an estimated two million people present, though no one could really count them. The pope was celebrating the nine hundredth anniversary of the martyrdom of St. Stanislas. Though 8 May was the official date for the celebration, the government had refused the pope permission to come at that time, imagining that there could be political provocation in the feast. But the pope had used his papal privilege to postpone the celebrations until his visit. Yet he was no longer in a mood to challenge anyone and clearly wanted his visit to end amicably. He thanked the government for having welcomed him, described his visit as "an act of courage by both sides," and declared that the Church was not concerned with "Christian imperialism" but rather with "service." But once again, he made a plea to "open wide the frontiers." His last words in Poland, after he had kissed the soil at Kraków airport, were: "I say farewell to Poland, to my motherland, to this country from which my heart can never be parted." Then he flew off, just before six o'clock, back to the "universal solicitude of all the churches," this time in a LOT plane.

THE SIGNIFICANCE OF THE POPE'S VISIT TO POLAND

It is easier to record the outline of the pope's visit to Poland and to quote his sermons than to say exactly what it meant. It was a parable in action. John Paul II, while remaining always courteous and refusing facile demagogy, had spoken with great and surprising freedom. It was almost as though he did not expect to return to Poland in the foreseeable future and had said all he had to say. He had dared to put into words what most Poles feel but cannot publicly say. To that extent he had behaved more like a prophet than a diplomat. "He came here like Moses," said one Pole, not normally given to hyperbole. The most indubitable effect of his visit was that it boosted the morale of the Polish Church and, insofar as the Church is only with difficulty separated from the nation, of the nation as well. From the government's point of view it distracted attention from the grave economic crisis.

But there was something else and something more fundamental. Why, after 455 years of Italian dominance, should there be a Polish pope? The answer lies deep in the mystery of divine providence, but the pope himself had pondered this question. He suggested a partial answer in his sermon in Victory Square, Warsaw. "Have we not the right," he said, "to think that one must come to this very place, to this land, along these roads, in order to read again the witness of Christ's cross and resurrection?" Though it was a question and not an infallible pronouncement, the majority of Poles are convinced that the election of a Polish pope was some compensation for the sufferings of partition and occupation that had been inflicted upon the nation. They distinguish between the "nation" (or people) and the state. The pope in Poland let his heart speak, and the people responded.

Though political calculations may have been far from his mind, and though he repeatedly asserted that his visit had a purely religious motive, there were undoubtedly political effects. The Church had demonstrated its strength, its self-discipline, and its rootedness among the ordinary people. Atheism is unnatural in Poland, whatever the official ideology proclaims. The Church may be able to exploit all this in its future negotiations with the government. The farewell speech of President Jabłonski at Kraków airport suggested that the government was putting a brave front on things, was desperately trying to interpret the visit in as positive a way as possible, and stressing the "points of convergence." No doubt this is the right tactical approach: it ensures that the government does not appear to have suffered a reverse. The pope embraced Jabłonski warmly at Kraków airport—much more warmly and spontaneously than on his arrival in Warsaw.

Yet it would be naive to imagine that nothing has changed in Poland or that the Pope's visit simply confirmed the *status quo*. The cautious step by step *Ostpolitik* practiced in the pontificate of Paul VI has given way to a bold and imaginative policy which simply refuses to admit that the countries which happen to live under what is known as "socialism" are not part of a wider Europe. As a Pole, who knows the situation and knows just how hard to push, the pope can rush in where others would rightly fear to tread. He took a deliberate risk. He spoke the truth, even when it was unwelcome. Stalinist hard-liners are not an extinct species in Poland, and one of them was heard to complain that "the pope's visit has undone all our work over the last thirty-five years." Much—indeed everything—depends on whether the "friendly ally," the Soviet Union, leaves the Poles to settle their own affairs.

The whole visit was very characteristic of John Paul II. Intelligence and instinct combined to lead him to act as he did, leaving the unpredictable consequences in the hands of God. What is absolutely certain is that he injected a new factor into Polish social life, and that nothing can be the same in the future.

BACK IN ROME: QUO VADIS?

Along the Via della Riconciliazione, Mussolini's "Reconciliation Street" running from the Tiber to St. Peter's Square, red posters welcomed the homecoming "Worker-Pope from the People's Democracy of Poland." The preceding autumn, in the same place, and again on a red background, the signs had read "We want a Catholic pope!" That poster was signed by a group on the radical Right who were showing that they considered the deceased Paul VI as scarcely more than a loyal Catholic and nevertheless wished him a "lenient sentence." The present greetings came from the opposite side; the welcoming poster was signed "Christians for Socialism." Was this an attempt at unity? An outstretched hand? An appeal: What is right in Poland should also be fairplay in Italy?

The pope's reaction to the Italian milieu—with its polarization, its terror tactics, the coexistence of the Communist and Christian Democratic parties, and the cropping-up of old and new splinter parties—was, in the first months, rather relaxed. "As a foreigner he will not involve himself in our politics" was the positive comment one frequently heard in the early days of his pontificate. Other persons expressed the same idea more symbolically: "The Tiber has grown wider." Nor did his choice of Archbishop Casaroli to be Cardinal–Secretary of State disappoint these expectations. For Casaroli, although an Italian, had scarcely concerned himself with his country while working under Pope Paul. He was instead responsible for the so-called *Ostpolitik* (the Vatican's policies in Eastern Europe), which made him a controversial figure in Poland, among other places. Now, immediately after returning to Rome, John Paul II presented Casaroli to the public, in no uncertain terms, as his principal co-worker. This has generally been interpreted as a sign of continuity with the Vatican's foregoing "foreign policy," which also includes the negotiations for the overdue revision of the Concordat with Italy that was concluded under Mussolini fifty years ago.

And what of internal Church politics? Paul VI, except during his last year, had governed with a strong "minister of the interior," or so-called *Sostituto,* in the person of G. Benelli, (now cardinal in Florence), and through Benelli had further centralized the bureaucratic machinery of the Church's head office. Benelli was not averse to mixing in Italian politics and kept a watchful eye on the Italian Church and its Bishops' Conference. John Paul has given this Conference a young and dynamic chairman in the person of Archbishop Ballestrero (Turin), and at the same time has appointed a Spaniard, Monsignor Martinez Somalo, to the post of Substitute/Sostituto. All this implies that he prefers to see the Italian Church in future governed with less dependence on the Vatican. On the other hand, John Paul II does not shrink from making appeals to Italian popular morality or from emphasizing the Church's share of responsibility for the conduct of public life. The new pope can afford to do so, because he is already extremely popular with the Italians. The crowds that flock to the pope's General Audience Wednesday after Wednesday, flooding St. Peter's Square, choking traffic with their busses, and setting new records for the purchase of papal portraits, include a high percentage of Italians from every corner of the peninsula.

One characteristic feature of the pope's administrative style would appear to be a truly personal commitment to the role of Bishop of Rome. It remains to be seen how the direction of the *worldwide* Church will take shape in his pontificate. Some people are hoping that he will give greater weight to the bishop's synods and perhaps even grant their periodic "Councils" a place in his administration. In any case, a member of this Council mentioned, in a letter to the author, his conviction that this pope would not "retreat to an ivory tower in order to receive the emanations of the Holy Spirit"; but instead he will pay attention to the bishops and the whole Church. And where this question of "collegiality" and bishops' synods is concerned, Archbishop Helder-Camâra, whose sights are constantly set on the future, voiced an equal conviction: "Rest assured, you will have cause for rejoicing yet!"

"Quo vadis, Domine"—"Where are you going, Lord?" According to tradition, St. Peter in his flight from Rome was met by a vision of Christ, to whom he addressed this question. The answer sent him back into the Imperial City: there Christ was to be crucified again. John Paul II recalled this legend in his inauguration homily, citing as well the novel *Quo Vadis,* by the Polish writer Henryk Sienkiewicz, about the conflict between Christianity and the Roman Empire.

CHRONOLOGY OF IMPORTANT DATES

This schematic biography of Karol Wojtyła presents the major dates and events in relation to political developments, particularly those occurring in Poland.

BENEDICT XV   1914–22

1920

Karol Josef Wojtyła is born in Wadowice, Poland, on 18 May. He grows up in a period of confusion and anguish. World War I and the enduring conflicts with Russia have brought Poland to the brink of destruction. The worldwide Depression hits Poland hard, and in 1926 Piłsudski's iron hand changes the fragile democracy into a total dictatorship.

Reforms are initiated by Pope Benedict XV with the goal of

PIUS XI   1922–39

1938

On completing his secondary schooling (with awarding of the baccalaureate), Wojtyła enters the Jagiellonian University in Kraków. He studies Polish literature and is one of the founders of the student theater group "Studio 39."

During the war Wojtyła works for the Solvay mines and chemical works. At the same time he joins with Kotlarczyk to organize the Rhapsodic Theater in Kraków. Sought by the Nazis, he is hidden

PIUS XII   1939–58

1942

Extension of the Nazi racial legislation over all areas occupied by Germany.

1943

Jewish uprising in the Warsaw ghetto.

1944

Allied landing in Normandy.

The registration of Wojtyła's birth in the presbytery of Wadowice. The record, kept in Latin, notes the major events of his life, including baptism, confirmation, ordination, consecration as bishop and cardinal, and at the very bottom, his election as Pope John Paul II, dated "16.X.1978."

Metryka urodzonych.

easing the strain of conflicting nationalisms. His clearness of thought, cool political instinct, and love for his fellow man, particularly for the victims of the war, help him as a mediator during the war. His successor, Pius XI, proves to be a scholarly, critical man who detects Hitler's true aims quite early.

1921

Riga peace conference.

1933

Beginning of Hitler's reign □.
Pope Pius XI refuses to receive Hitler in the Vatican and leaves the Holy City in protest. During the final years of his pontificate he uses all the weight of his position to try to ease suffering.

by Archbishop Sapieha. During these years he resolves to become a priest and begins his theological studies.

On the death of Pius XI in 1939, Eugenio Pacelli (Pius XII) succeeds him as pontiff. His pontificate will last two decades.

1939

Invasion of Poland by the Germans. Outbreak of World War II. Poland is partitioned for the fourth time in her history.

1945

Germany surrenders. The Yalta Conference is convened.
Hiroshima and Nagasaki are destroyed by atomic bombing □.
End of World War II.
Founding session of the United Nations Organization.

□ This symbol in the text refers to illustrations.

122

1946

Wojtyła is ordained a priest and, the same year, sent to Rome for further studies at the Dominican Angelicum seminary.

1947

At the war's end, Poland has two *de facto* governments: one capitalist-bourgeois, and one Communist. Gomułka's "Democratic Bloc" wins in the first elections. His successor, Bołeslaw Bierut, becomes the first postwar president of Poland. Under his reign a severe process of Stalinization is instituted, and will continue even after Bierut's death in 1953.

1948

Wojtyła completes his studies in Rome with a dissertation on the Spanish mystic St. John of the Cross. The same year, he returns to Poland, becomes vicar in Niegowic, and then is named priest in a parish in Kraków. The Communist regime uses all its power to break the Church's opposition and in the years 1948–1952 condemns several priests to death.

1950

Pope Pius XII officially proclaims the dogma of the Assumption of Mary into heaven. Conflicts between Polish Church and state reach a crisis in 1953. Sapieha, having been named a cardinal, dies in 1951. His successor, Archbishop Baziak, is removed by the regime after a rigged "show" trial. After repeated outspoken criticisms of the government's policies, Cardinal Wyszyński is placed under house arrest. Wojtyła, intending to begin a professorial career, prepares for the qualification examination. He teaches ethics at the Kraków Seminary, and on the closing of the university there in 1954, transfers to the Catholic University in Lublin.

1956

Hungarian uprising □. Police and army join the fight on the side of the people. On Gerö's appeal, Soviet military units attack Budapest. Cardinal Josef Mindszenty is freed by the rebels and once again takes up residence in the Bishop's Palace. Imre Nagy becomes the new prime minister. Gomułka returns to power in Poland and allows the church somewhat more leeway. The prominent Catholic newspaper *Tygodnik Powszechny* resumes publication.

1958

On 4 July in Warsaw, Wojtyła is consecrated bishop. As assistant to Archbishop Baziak of Kraków, the young bishop is now involved in the heart of Polish Church politics.

JOHN XXIII   1958–63

Death of Pope Pius XII. A new period for the Roman Catholic Church begins under Pope John XXIII: an opening on the world, a concern with all men regardless of their religion or race. The pope's legacy is exemplified in the Second Vatican Council and his encyclical *Pacem in Terris*. In this document the pope supports democracy, the right to resist social injustice, workers' rights, women's equality, the rights of minorities and all victims of dis-

crimination, disarmament, and aid to economically underdeveloped countries.

1961

Bishop Wojtyła works in the central administration of the Polish Church and prepares for new duties as successor to Archbishop Baziak. After migrations and flights from East Germany reach a new peak in 1961, a dangerous critical point in East-West relations is reached with the closing off of all traffic between the two halves of the city. The Western nations

PAUL VI   1963–78

react with protests and popular demonstrations, which are powerless to halt the construction of the Berlin wall which makes flight mortally dangerous if not impossible □.
The wall becomes a dramatic symbol for the division of the world into eastern and western blocs.

1962

Bishop Wojtyła is named as successor to Baziak in Kraków. Opening of the Second Vatican Council, the greatest gathering in the history of the Church. During the Council, Bishop Wojtyła is active on the committee for the study of marriage. "It is the principal task of this Council to preserve and to explain the sacred tradition of the Christian Church. This teaching embraces the whole person, who consists of body and soul; and all of us living on this earth are called, as pilgrims, to set our sights on our heavenly fatherland" (John XXIII).
Paul VI, Giovanni Battista Montini, succeeds Pope John XXIII, 1963.

1964

Wojtyła is named archbishop.

1967

Pope Paul VI makes Archbishop Karol Wojtyła a cardinal. Wojtyła thus becomes the number-two man (after Wyszyński) in the hierarchy of the Polish Church. As cardinal he takes frequent risks, protesting vehemently every time the government oversteps its prerogatives.
"It is intolerable that a group of men should compel a whole people to an ideology, a conviction, that goes against the beliefs of the majority. Christians must

JOHN PAUL I   1978

arm themselves against the dangers of the society that surrounds them, so that they can become true members of the Church, for the state is seeking to create a breed of person who will only serve its own interests" (Cardinal Karol Wojtyła).

Pope Paul VI carries the Council forward in the spirit of John XXIII. But in moral theology he draws narrower limits than his predecessor had done. In 1967 he publishes two encyclicals: *Populorum Progressio* and *Sacerdotalis Coelibatus.*

1968

Publication of a third encyclical, *Humanae Vitae,* concerning respect for the unborn foetus and the policy on birth control. One year later Cardinal Wojtyła publishes a theological commentary on the encyclical which staunchly defend's the pope's viewpoint.

After a period of opening toward the West in Czechoslovakia, which also gave hope to the other Eastern European countries, the Czechs are invaded by Soviet, East German, Polish, Hungarian, and Bul-

garian troops, and the "Prague Spring" comes to a violent end □. Leaders of the Czech reforms, Swoboda, Dubcek, Smrkowsky, Kriegel, and Cernik, are forced to sign an agreement with Moscow which will have far-reaching effects for the Eastern Bloc in its conduct toward Moscow. In order to avoid a similar armed intervention, careful measures are taken in Poland.

During this time Cardinal Wojtyła actively involves himself in international Church affairs. He takes part in the Bishops' Synod in Rome in 1971 and speaks out unequivocally for priestly celibacy. In 1974 he is named to the council of the general secretariat of the Synod.

After his fifteen-year asylum in the United States embassy in Budapest, Hungary's primate, Cardinal Mindszenty, leaves his homeland in 1971 after urging by Pope Paul VI and travels to Rome. He joins the pope in opening the largest Bishops' Synod in the history of the Church □.

Pope Paul VI dies on 6 August 1978. After an extremely short conclave, Albino Luciani, John

Paul I, is elected as the new pope. But just a month after taking office, the pope dies of a heart attack, leaving an enduring memory even after so short a time.

16 October 1978

Karol Wojtyła is elected pope. In his enthronement ceremony John Paul II breaks with the Vatican tradition: he addresses his greeting in several languages to the jubilant crowds outdoors in St. Peter's Square. In January 1979 the pope attends the Bishops Conference of the Latin American Church in Puebla, Mexico. In June John Paul II makes a triumphant journey to Poland.

After his election, the "foreign" Pope John Paul II first won the hearts of the Italians, and then those of people all over the world.

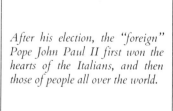

ACKNOWLEDGMENTS

The English translations of poems by Karol Wojtyła on pages 26, 47, and 68–69, are quoted from *Easter Vigil and Other Poems,* © Libreria Editrice Vaticana, Vatican City, 1979, translation © Jerzy Peterkiewicz, 1979, first published in English by Hutchinson and Company, London, 1979, and quoted by permission.

The text in this book was written by:

Dr. Ludwig Kaufmann S.J.:
Pages: 6, 7, 8, 10 11, 13, 30, 58, 59, 92, 93, 94, 95, 96, 97, 98, 100, 101, 102, 104, 105, 121.

Dr. Peter Hebblethwaite:
Pages: 14, 15, 16, 22, 24, 28, 34, 36, 38, 40, 41, 42, 43, 44, 45, 46, 47, 48, 54, 60, 64, 68, 70, 72, 74, 76, 80, 82, 84, 88, 89, 91, 106, 107, 108, 109, 110, 112, 113, 114, 115, 116, 120.

Dr. Reinhold Lehmann:
Pages 66, 67

The captions were written by:

Dr. Alois Anklin and Dr. Ludwig Kaufmann

Additional material, and English translations, by the McGraw-Hill editorial staff.

INDEX